In Defense of
HYPOCRISY

Picking Sides in the War on Virtue

JEREMY LOTT

NELSON CURRENT

A Subsidiary of Thomas Nelson, Inc.

Published in Nashville, Tennessee, by Nelson Current, a division of a wholly-owned subsidiary (Nelson Communications, Inc.) of Thomas Nelson, Inc.

Nelson Current books may be purchased in bulk for educational, business, fundraising, or sales promotional use. For information, please e-mail SpecialMarkets@ThomasNelson.com.

**Library of Congress Cataloging-in-Publication data on file
with the Library of Congress.**

ISBN 1-59555-052-6

Printed in the United States of America

06 07 08 09 10 QW 5 4 3 2 1

To Reverend Robert Lott,
whose hypocrisies are microscopic

You call yourself a Christian
I think that you're a hypocrite.
MICK JAGGER

We are not hypocrites in our sleep.
WILLIAM HAZLITT

CONTENTS

1

BILL BENNETT'S RAP SHEET

Sounds to me like you're an opportunistic hypocritical little pudnocker.

COLONEL FLAGG

I was tipped off by an excited *Washington Monthly* hand that his low-circulation magazine was about to break a major story, jointly, with *Newsweek*. It was the spring of 2003. The subject of the exposé was former education secretary, drug czar, and *New York Times* best-selling author William J. Bennett.[1]

The scoop was this: the author of *The Book of Virtues* had bet millions of dollars in book royalties and speaking fees at casinos in Las Vegas and Atlantic City. His preferred games of chance were video poker and high-stakes slot machines. Bennett was such a high roller that most casinos would send a limo, put him up for a few nights on the house, and turn him loose in the high-limit rooms.

By most accounts, the casinos got a good return on their investment. Bennett would hope for digital straight flushes or wrestle with one-armed bandits into the wee hours of the morning, at a cost of $100 to $500 a pull. Several casinos extended lines of credit in excess of $200,000, and those often failed to contain the damage. Internal documents reveal that, in one two-month period, Bennett was forced to wire more than $1.4 million to cover his losses.

When he was informed that the magazines were taking the story public, Bennett agreed to talk with *Newsweek*'s Jonathan Alter. He claimed his luck was not nearly so bad as the Dorian Gray-like portrait that a nongambler might sketch after peeking at casino documents. Bennett elaborated, "You can roll up and down a lot in one day, as we have on many occasions. You may cycle several hundred thousand dollars in an evening and net out only a few thousand." In fact, he puffed up his chest and claimed that over the last decade he'd "come out fairly close to even."

That "fairly close to even" line was soon to be much mocked in the press, but Bennett soldiered on. He worked the high-limit rooms and preferred automated games of chance because he found the alternative annoying. "When I go to the tables," he explained, "people talk—and they want to talk about politics. I don't want that. I do this for three hours to relax." Message: who could begrudge the guy a little relaxation?

Bennett argued that his behavior was not wrong for three reasons. One, he could afford it. He didn't "play the milk money," as he put it. He obeyed the laws, paid his taxes, reported any winnings, and flossed twice a day. Two, he didn't lie about it, except in a genial, size-of-that-fish sort of way. The *Washington Times* had reported on his gambling in two separate stories, one about a jackpot that he'd hit while playing slots at the Bellagio in

Las Vegas.[2] Three, gambling is not a sin, so long as it does not harm others.

"I've gambled all my life and it's never been a moral issue with me. I liked church bingo when I was growing up. I've been a poker player," Bennett told *Newsweek*. When it was put to him that gambling is a pathological addiction for some people, he denied being a problem gambler. Bennett fit gaming into the same moral category as alcohol: "If you can't handle it, don't do it."

As damage control strategies go, Bennett's approach was sound and, for all we know, heartfelt. He came across as a regular guy who wanted to unwind for a few hours, avoid tedious arguments about politics, and maybe nurse a bourbon on the rocks while he put a bit of his own money on the line.

At the same time, the magazine writers were coming off as scolds and worse. They had relied on leaked documents from casinos to take a shot at a man because of his political beliefs. The *Washington Monthly* framed the story as payback: Bennett had criticized President Clinton during the impeachment fracas of the late '90s—in fact, he even "gambled throughout Clinton's impeachment"—so he was now fair game.[3] He had spoken out against gay marriage, abortion, and crack cocaine so it made good sense to expose his private casino receipts to the light of day.

What's more, the journalists didn't have the goods, and they knew it. Joshua Green, principal author of the *Monthly* story, closed it out with this feather of a punch: "By furtively indulging in a costly vice that destroys millions of lives and families across the nation, Bennett has profoundly undermined the credibility of his word on this moral issue." My loose translation: Bill

3

Bennett is not as outraged as we are about gambling. He even plays the slots himself. How dare he.

So they tried to bait Bennett into responding. *Newsweek* editor Mark Whitaker closed his editor's note for the issue by opining, "It appears . . . the conservative former Education secretary who makes a living writing about 'virtue'"—note the scare quotes—"has a little vice." He called the story a reminder that moralists "always seem to have an easier time lecturing others about behavior than controlling their own."[4]

Green assured readers of the *Las Vegas Business Press* that other high rollers could relax because this was a onetime thing. Their target had been a "national scold" who "threw stones while he was living in a glass house."[5] It was the journalists' job to expose the former drug czar, but there the scorched-roulette campaign would end. As long as gamblers stayed at the tables and didn't hold forth on moral issues on CNN, they had little to fear from the muckrakers.

That was an astounding concession. Green was endorsing the *omertà*-like code of the numbers industry, with one important modification. He was saying that what happens in Vegas stays in Vegas, unless it happens to Bill Bennett.

"I'M NOT A HYPOCRITE"

Once the story broke, talking heads couldn't stop talking about Bennett's alleged hypocrisy. Bennett maintained that his gambling did not fall under the modern use of the term. For him, games of chance were never a "moral issue," and he had never spoken out against gambling *qua* gambling. He told interviewer Tim Russert that he hadn't taken to his soapbox on this subject and so any contradictions were put there by his detractors. "I'm not a hypocrite," Bennett said, over a month after the story broke.[6]

His critics were not persuaded and probably not persuadable. Writing in the online magazine *Slate*, Michael Kinsley tore into the noncontradiction defense. That he had never condemned gambling, Kinsley wrote, "doesn't show that Bennett is not a hypocrite. It just shows that he's not a complete idiot." Then Kinsley decided to channel the spirit of the great Dana Carvey *Saturday Night Live* character Church Lady: "Working his way down the list of other people's pleasures, weaknesses, and uses of American freedom, [Bennett] just happened to skip over his own. How convenient."[7]

As went Kinsley, so went the tidal wave of respectable opinion. Because of the left-right format of most political television chat shows, many conservatives who are not gung-ho about gambling found themselves having to defend a high roller against charges of hypocrisy. This mismatch produced some comical results. On *Crossfire*, former Clinton administration flack Paul Begala used the Gospel of Matthew (or as he put it "the book of St. Matthews") to Bible-thump an evangelical Christian rival over Bennett's supposed moral laxity.[8]

In the weekly opinion magazine *The Nation*, Katha Pollitt expressed a fairly common liberal complaint about *l'affaire* Bennett. She wished it "had been sex, maybe some of that hot 'man on dog' action that Senator Rick Santorum is so keen on chatting about." However, she decided that since the target of the exposé had been Bennett, the "thundering sultan of sanctimony" himself, high stakes gambling would "do quite nicely."[9]

Thus did the end (getting that bastard Bill Bennett) more than justify the means (digging through private casino records and publishing the results) that might otherwise have troubled sensitive progressive souls. But the same people who are normally fierce advocates of privacy and civil liberties were too busy piling on to notice. Here was a chance to kick a former drug czar when he was down, to censor a critic of rap music, yo. That sort of opportunity doesn't come along every day. As an added bonus, they could call Bennett a sucker, a loser, a whale.

The condemnations grew so loud and numerous that Bennett's old colleague and supporter William F. Buckley, Jr. weighed in with "discouraging commentary." Buckley wrote in his nationally syndicated column that Bennett "is through."[10] His role in public life would be nil. No Republican administration would hire him. Book sales would dry up. The future he had to look forward to did not include playing the slots because he would need that money to buy milk for the wife and kids.

The "he's through" view was a decent reflection of the evolving thought of America's pundits and journalists. Many critics either predicted or openly wished that his gambling losses would also cost Bennett the position he had carved out for himself as Mr. Morality, or, to use Buckley's more marbled phrase, as "the nation's premier secular catechist of virtue."

Predictions of Bennett's demise rested on three questionable assumptions that fall over like dominos on closer inspection. The first was that Bennett was, in fact, a hypocrite. The second, that his hypocrisy would matter, that it would rob his words of any authority. The third assumption: Bennett's audience would view the matter of his outing as a one-sided affair, with Bennett wearing the hypocritical horns and the chattering class sporting the halos. In fact, as I have already hinted, the whole episode was shot through with hypocrisy. Not that there's anything wrong with that.

DEFINING THE MILK MONEY DOWN

That so many people were quick to label Bennett a hypocrite is a bit of a puzzlement. The *American Heritage Dictionary* is a pretty good bellwether of modern English usage. According to the most recent edition, hypocrisy is "the professing of beliefs or virtues one does not possess."[11] Bennett never believed, and certainly never professed to believe, that gambling is wrong. He never spoke out against it or tried especially hard to hide the fact that he gambled. Therefore, Bill Bennett is not a hypocrite. Case dismissed.

Not so fast, said many of his old sparring partners. Beliefs are one thing, virtues another. Virtues are eternal and woven together like a sweater. Yank out one thread and you ruin the whole thing. As Michael Kinsley put the question, "Is there some reason why [Bennett's] general intolerance of the standard vices does not apply to this one? None that he's ever mentioned."[12]

Actually, there was one really big reason, one that Bennett had mentioned repeatedly. Maybe Kinsley was too busy blasting away to comprehend it. Kinsley accused him of "spraying smarm" for divulging that he had started gambling with church bingo, but Bennett wasn't just blowing hot saliva-flecked air. He was offering an explanation. Bennett is Catholic, and his understanding of right and wrong is informed and bounded by his religious tradition.

Bennett's religion is relevant because Catholicism envisions a more muscular role for a secular authority than, say, conservative strains of Protestantism, and it places a premium on being a law-abiding citizen. Case in point: the confessional gets mighty uncomfortable as every April fifteenth approaches and a number of priests decide to ask if you have cheated on your taxes. (Best answer: "Well, father, you'll have to talk to my Jewish accountant.")

Within the boundaries of what is legal, however, Bennett's church (and mine) tends to be fairly lenient with the thou-shalt-nots. The use of marijuana and cocaine is a no-no, but alcohol and tobacco are permitted and then some. In cities with large ethnic Catholic populations, it isn't uncommon to go to a pub and find a priest, in his jacket and collar, belly up to the bar, pounding back the pints and lighting up coffin nails.

Granted, there are limits. All good Catholics are supposed to stop short of serious drunkenness, and they are encouraged to give such things up for the Lenten season leading up to Easter and certain holy days. But the rule, which runs counter to most stereotypes of the Catholic Church, is moderation and toleration rather than prohibition and repression.

So it is with gaming. According to the Catechism, gambling is A-OK as long as the gamblers don't play the grocery money. "Games of chance (card games, etc.) or wagers," you see, "are not in themselves contrary to justice. They become morally unacceptable when they deprive someone of what is necessary to provide for his needs and those of others." The theologians do warn that the "passion" for gambling can become dangerous, but they reserve their heavy fire for the cheats and sharks: "Unfair wagers and cheating at games constitute grave matter."[13]

Rome may be wrong about matters grave and small, but the vision that Bennett had put forward, and the standard against which it would have been appropriate to judge him, was a lay Catholic's vision of the good life. Bennett's ideal man worked hard, paid his taxes, raised a family, went to church, gave to charity, involved himself in the community, and unwound in ways that enjoy the sanction of law and are within his means. And Bennett's means were considerable enough that $500 a pull did not place him outside this model.

Here's the point: Bennett was not gerrymandering a list of vices to exclude things that he enjoys. He was enjoying activities that church and society had taught him to regard as perfectly acceptable. The thing that was selective here was not Bennett's notion of hypocrisy but his opponents' preconceived notions of virtue. They viewed him as the no-fun guy, so evidence of fun was proof positive of his hypocrisy.

Now, you don't have to be a fan of Bennett to question whether his opponents were being remotely fair, or remotely reasonable. And you need not endorse, say, his views on abortion or drugs or rap music to wonder at this point if this whole hypocrisy thing has gotten a bit out of hand.

SHUT UP, THEY EXPLAINED

I have focused on the case of Bill Bennett so far because it's what golfers call a sure shot: a short putt from the green with no slope, no wind, next to no chance of missing. A gimme. Here was a man whose gambling losses were exposed largely because his political opponents wanted payback. Then, rather than argue with him, critics went to town on a straw man that was shaped vaguely like Bennett. He was a hypocrite because, well, because they wished it so. And this counterfeited hypocrisy was introduced as evidence that no one should take him seriously anymore. A columnist for the *Orlando Sentinel* complained, "If you're peddling virtue . . . you can't very well indulge in a vice."[14]

Read that last sentence again. It demonstrates perfectly a point of view that some wag might call the "saint or shut up" approach to hypocrisy. That is, if you are the Pope, Billy Graham, Jimmy Carter, Mother Teresa, Mister Rogers, or the Dalai Lama, you can talk. We will listen, though often grudgingly, to what you have to say on moral matters. Otherwise, we don't want to hear it. Take it to a Gamblers Anonymous meeting. Maybe the recovering poker fiends will care.

A few brave skeptics have raised objections to the "saint or shut up" formula. The most convincing criticism comes from human nature itself. People who exhibit one or more vices—in religious language, sinners—make up the bulk of the world's population. Yet experience tells us that those people who have vices usually also model better qualities, or virtues. If a man's behavior is usually but not always admirable, does that disqualify him from speaking on moral issues? Should a single sin be enough to expel the would-be virtue peddler from the garden of polite opinion?

Ten years ago, political essayist Ramesh Ponnuru took up these questions for an article that ran in the Washington, D.C.-

based conservative magazine *The Weekly Standard* under the catchy headline "In Defense of Hypocrisy."[15] The backdrop for the essay was the outing of a political consultant as a prostitute-hiring toe sucker, but the analysis doesn't seem to have aged a nanosecond. In many ways, Ponnuru's words seem *more* relevant now in our post-9/11, post-Enron, post-Katrina world.

Brief flashback: Dick Morris was the Karl Rove of the 1990s, a talented political operator who secured a sitting president's reelection. Morris had worked with Bill Clinton from early in the future president's career in Arkansas politics. He helped Clinton claw his way back into the governor's mansion in 1982 after a humiliating defeat, and he was handed the task of rehabilitating the president after the '94 midterm elections washed Clinton's party out of both branches of Congress.

By following Morris's counsel, Clinton bloodied the new Republican majority in Congress. He signed welfare reform and anti-gay-marriage legislation, which took a few big social issues out of play. He paid lip service to the antigovernment anger that had stung his own party by announcing in his next State of the Union Address that the "era of big government is over." He used popular fears about deficits to beat back tax cuts. Taking a cue from Morris's extensive polling, Clinton told middle America that the Grand Old Party-poopers wanted to cancel their Medicare, repeal Medicaid, defund schools, and dump toxins into lakes and streams.

The about-faces and the attacks infuriated Republicans, but they did the trick for Clinton's electoral prospects. Morris successfully repositioned (or "triangulated," as he likes to call it) his candidate as a socially sane, fiscally prudent champion of solid middle-class concerns against left-wing nutters and moneyed interests. So there was an awful lot of gloating by Republicans, with charges of hypocrisy sprinkled liberally, when the supermarket tabloid *The Star* reported that Morris had hired a $200-an-hour call girl named Sherry Rowlands.[16]

Rowlands stressed that she had come forward with this information with no prompting from Republicans. Two of her allegations received wide circulation and forced Morris to step down from his official advisory role to the White House. One, Morris had a particularly embarrassing foot fetish. Two, he liked to pillow talk about his connection with Clinton. Morris read Rowlands excerpts of a speech that the president had yet to deliver, and he called Clinton at his private residence and put the conversation on the speakerphone to impress his "date."

According to Ponnuru, Morris's Republican critics had accused the political consultant of hypocrisy because he helped sell President Clinton "as a family-values candidate while [Morris was] conducting an affair with the founder of A Woman's Personal Touch cleaning service."[17] Ponnuru didn't argue with the charge that Morris was a hypocrite, but he pleaded with readers to cut hypocrisy some slack.

Since he was writing to a conservative audience, Ponnuru defended hypocrisy by appealing to self-preservation and shared principles. Right wingers should think twice before joining the antihypocritical pile-on, he argued, because moralistic Republicans are more susceptible to hypocrisy allegations than most politicians. Reports of philandering would not put much of a dent in the reputation of, say, Ted Kennedy, but they just might end the career of a Rick Santorum or a Dan Quayle.

That difference was unfortunate, he wrote, because if only saints are allowed to speak up for virtue then virtue is likely to be quickly shouted down. "Hypocrisy," Ponnuru explained, "serves an important social function." It allows us to retain moral standards even when we fail to measure up to those ideals. Then he pressed the claim even further: "For a society to be both decent and tolerable *requires* a healthy amount of hypocrisy."[18]

Ponnuru called the "saint or shut up" standard "in effect, a political weapon deployed solely against those who seek to raise public standards of morality." But framing the issue for a politically conservative audience caused him to take a too-narrow view. Moralists may be more vulnerable to charges of hypocrisy than, say, nihilists, but Dick Morris was no moralist. Neither are many of the people who stutter to defend themselves when faced with accusations of hypocrisy today.

"WE MAKE UP ISSUES"

In 1999, Clint Eastwood's *True Crime* was released in theaters to critical acclaim. The movie is a yarn about journalist Steve Everett's race to beat the clock. At midnight, San Quentin inmate Frank Louis Beechum (played by a saintly Isaiah Washington) is set to die by lethal injection. Everett (Eastwood), a veteran investigative reporter whose boozing and womanizing have nearly washed him out of the news biz, comes to believe Beechum is innocent. He has to fight against the law, public opinion, his own wife, and a brutal deadline to prove it.

But first Everett has to land the assignment, and that story is at least as interesting as the rest of the film. The reporter who had been set to do the final interview with Beechum for the *Oakland Tribune* unexpectedly dies in a car crash. The vacancy leads to heated words between the paper's young, new idealistic editor (Bob Findley, played by Dennis Leary) and its jaded middle-aged owner (James Woods as Alan Mann) over whether to stick Everett on the beat.

> **Findley:** The point is, this is not a Steve Everett slash-and-burn job, OK? This is a sidebar. It's an issue piece.
>
> **Mann:** *Oooh* (throat noises), an "issue piece." Well, dog my cats!
>
> **Findley:** This is capital punishment, Alan, OK? We are putting a man to death tonight. We are *killing* a *human being*.
>
> **Mann:** Oh, well, stop the presses. Jeez. Hey, by the way, Bob, that Amy what's-her-name—you know, the pregnant broad that old Frankie *shot* in the throat—was she a human being? Huh? Is that part of the issue?
>
> **Findley:** Yeah, OK, that is part of the issue.
>
> **Mann:** Bob, let me tell you something. Crumb cake?
>
> **Findley:** (Taken aback.) No.
>
> **Mann:** OK. Issues are shit that we make up to give ourselves an excuse to run good stories, *OK*? Judge grabs a female attorney's tits, hey, that's

the sex discrimination *"issue."* Nine-year-old
blows away his brother with an Uzi, the child
violence *"issue."* People want to read about sex
organs and blood, OK? We make up issues so
they don't have to feel too nasty about it, got it?

Findley: Then I might as well call Steve Everett now
because that's his attitude exactly.[19]

The newspaper owner character's snap judgment may have been
over the top, but that doesn't mean it was wrong. There are
many genuine issues pieces in newspapers and magazines today,
but often the "issue" simply serves as a way to tart up a scoop
that you would normally read alongside "Wolf Boy Joins the
Marines" and "Britney Spears Gives Birth" stories in the tabloid
section of the supermarket checkout line.

Tabloids are fearless and shameless. They expose things
because they understand that their audience wants to revel in the
details. When *The Star* broke the Dick Morris story, it didn't
attempt to explain why it was running the piece. It was a scoop
that would sell papers. Full stop. Justifications need not apply.

Newsweek and the *Washington Monthly* are different animals.
They think of themselves as respectable publications, and they
both produce editorial content with a more discriminating, non-
tabloid audience in mind. And so "Bill Bennett Loses Millions
Gambling" had to be wrapped in the "issue" of Bennett's supposed
moralistic contradictions. The small joke here was that both publications engaged in massive actual hypocrisy to break a story that
was about Bennett's fake hypocrisy.

Peter Beinart, then-editor of the centrist-liberal weekly magazine the *New Republic*, wasn't laughing. He was instead "dismayed" about a couple of things. He argued that journalists should have respected Bennett's privacy, and he took issue with "prominent liberals" who had decided to relax their normal pro-privacy standard "in order to help destroy [Bennett]." Beinart explained, "In exposing Bennett as a hypocrite, liberals need to make sure they don't expose themselves as well."[20]

"Too late" would be an understatement here, but it would also substitute a jab for the point this book is trying to make. For the last several years, I have earned my keep in the word trade. In Washington, D.C., and around the continent, I've bumped up against editors, publishers, reporters, freelancers, columnists, authors, cartoonists, proofreaders, and plain-vanilla writers. I'm usually "up" on the latest gossip and "down" with a few tricks of the trade. I even moonlighted as a bona fide media critic for a spell and was therefore forced to pay special attention to how the press actually works.

Here's a curiosity that a press critic has to scratch his head over all the time: When outsiders with no background in journalism look at a lot of the tricks that we use to gather and present news, they will often accuse us of hypocrisy. And, in the strictest sense, they are often right. A lot of what journalists do involves pretense. But those conventions seem a necessary part of the job, so we don't pay them much mind. The mental calculation seems to run:

hypocrisy = bad
journalism = good

How could one possibly have *anything* to do with the other?

I'M OK—YOU'RE A HYPOCRITE

The greatest obstacle in the way of making the case for hypocrisy is this: it's difficult to argue with a reflex. If you ask a man point-blank, "Are you a hypocrite?" his answer is unlikely to bear much of a relationship to the question you just put to him. He often hears, "Are you a bad person?" and answers *that* question instead. Few of us want to think of ourselves in such unflattering terms.

Critics who study closely the beliefs and actions of politicians, say, or journalists, will have an easy time finding all kinds of hypocrisy, real or imagined, to get worked up about. However they often put their own hypocrisies in different categories, or call them by different names, if they recognize them at all. Hypocrisy frequently involves self-deception.

Normally the best course would be to let sleeping assumptions lie, but I see the old grudging tolerance for hypocrisy eroding, and I worry. Make no mistake, the reason that we notice so much hypocrisy in the world around us is that it is there. The response of both the wannabe puritan and the modern liberal is to attack the hypocrisy, to go to work on the contradiction. But what if all that hypocrisy is there for a reason, maybe even a very good reason?

In Defense of Hypocrisy is an attempt to supply that reason. It might even introduce some novel twists to the discussion. The forces of hypocrisy tend to mount a narrow defense of the so-called vice. Yes, they say, hypocrisy is less than ideal and it has led to some horrible, indefensible outcomes, but it also helps to prop up moral norms and preserve useful fictions. And without those norms and those illusions, well, we'd have anarchy.

In the 2005 film *Lord of War,* antihero arms smuggler Yuri Orlov (Nicolas Cage) patiently explains to the federal agent who has finally busted him why the government is going to cut the old death merchant loose. On several occasions Orlov had dirtied his hands so that certain officials could make a show of keeping theirs clean. He admits to the earnest young agent that, sure, he may be evil, but "I'm a necessary evil."

Now, the usual apologists for hypocrisy have a point about that, one that I will explore and examine. But their defense doesn't get us all the way to where we need to go. It runs out of gas and we have to thumb it the rest of the way. It's past time for a defense that is sleeker, with less rough edges and better gas mileage. Call it Occam's Honda.

The long version of this argument will weave in and out of the rest of the book, but here it is in brief: Hypocrisy is so widespread that it might as well be part of our DNA. It is widespread because it is useful. It is useful for two reasons, one obvious and one that's a bit tricky.

While hypocrisy usually helps to prop up norms and preserve the existing order, that isn't always the case. It also provides a way for good men to pay lip service to heinous governments and warped social customs while working to thwart and ultimately undermine them.

You see, hypocrisy is not *just* a necessary evil. It's also an engine of moral progress.

***

A note to motivationally challenged readers: I'd prefer it if you read *In Defense of Hypocrisy* straight through, but it's your money and your time, so here's a cheat sheet. If you've no interest in examining hypocrisy in politics, start with the third chapter. If you don't want to know how hypocrisy works (its structure, history, use, and so forth), skip ahead to the fourth. No interest in hypocrisy and Christianity? On to the fifth! If hypocrisy in Hollywood doesn't float your boat, launch ahead to the sixth chapter. There you will learn, among other things, that intolerance of hypocrisy is causing many people to die painfully. Finally, I close with a Rodney King-like plea for a ceasefire in the hypocrisy wars. If that doesn't do it for you, give this book to your niece.

2

CONSERVATIVES AND CADS

Hypocrisy is a revolting, psychopathic state.

ANTON CHEKHOV

In January 2004, Dr. Anton Kris delivered a lecture in New York City at a meeting of the American Psychoanalytic Association. The subject of the talk was hypocrisy and what we might call gullibility. Kris, a professor of psychiatry from Harvard Medical School, spoke about why we are often fooled by the behavior of hypocrites.[1]

"Ladies and gentlemen," he said to the assembly of therapists, "we are all hypocritical about hypocrisy." People routinely condemn it and condone it without noticing the internal contradiction. We "hold hypocrisy in contempt," and yet we both expect and accept a certain amount of it. We even "applaud hypocritical accusations of hypocrisy" by politicians, so long as they happen to "share *our* views."

He explained that people are often fooled by hypocrites because they need to believe in *something*. The simplest way to understand their duped-ness, he said, is that the "desire for certainty" leads some to the "idealization of the hypocrite in exchange for the individual's credulity." The hypocrite represents himself as both certain and righteous, and so uncertain, unrighteous people are often more willing to trust him.

Then Kris dug down a bit. We tend to think of hypocrisy in terms of politics and religion, but it goes lower and taps into something deeper. The idea that some person or institution is "sufficiently powerful to dispel uncertainty," he said, is an important conceit for child rearing, education, medicine, and, yes, psychoanalysis.

The speaker cited examples from literature and film and then circled around to his own profession. He used unethical analysts and their long-suffering patients as grand examples of predatory hypocrites and the folks taken in by their behavior.

For instance, in one well-documented case an analyst "abruptly asked [a patient] for her sexual thoughts about him." He touched her cheek and in the next session asked her to "sit in his lap and began caressing and kissing her." When the patient asked if this was a normal part of treatment, the counselor replied that it was "in the literature," and the explanation appeared to put away her doubts. The affair lasted for several years and came to light only after the analyst had retired.

Kris was bothered by the fact that patients are often reluctant to stop seeing unethical, hypocritical analysts. Even after it is clear that something is grossly wrong with the normal doctor-client relationship, including childish or unreasonable demands or even sexual abuse, the patient will often stick it out with her analyst. She acquiesces against all available evidence, hoping that things

will improve, not unlike the battered wife who insists that she tripped down the stairs.

Kris told the audience that he had found the best way to get such a patient to end the relationship is to convince her to see another analyst in addition to the unethical one. The new analyst then works to wean her off of the bad analyst's larger-than-life presence and self-serving advice.

But why should that half-measure be necessary? he wondered. Why is it that patients who seem otherwise capable of holding down a job and getting along in life fail so badly when it comes to dealing with therapists who get out of line?

The reason is that they don't *want* to think badly of their analysts. A deep bond of trust is a necessary part of therapy, and it is prone to abuse by the more experienced party. When abuse occurs, patients have three options. First, there's the self-assertive option. Tell the good doctor to knock it off and stick to his mission to help you sort through your problems. Second is the legal option. Quit seeing the therapist and report his violations to a medical board or to the police.

But both of those scenarios are unappealing to many patients, and so they choose option number three by default. They allow their desire to continue the therapy—even once it has become abusive—to override their own good sense. A process that was meant to improve them and make them more independent instead diminishes them and makes them codependent. It warps their judgment.

Kris lamented that there is no adequate term for the party on the receiving end of hypocritical behavior. There are at least "two participants in hypocrisy," and our designated words *gull, dupe,*

and *victim* give the wrong impression of one of those parties. That is, the words "give the impression that there is a passive party," when it takes two to tango. One leads, the other follows.

He wasn't blaming the victim so much as trying to understand why certain people are more likely to receive abuse than others. The hypocrite, Kris concluded, "trades both on desire and on defense against the dread of uncertainty." The conditions that allow hypocritical snake oil salesmen to succeed come from impulses that are powerful and universal. It is not an exaggeration to say that a potential sucker is born every minute.

BRIDGES IN BROOKLYN

In politics, the hypocrite often poses as the righteous opponent of hypocrisy. A pitch-perfect case in point would be Howard Dean's appearance on *Meet the Press* in May of 2005. The recently elected chairman of the Democratic National Committee had been a controversial pick. He had been the early favorite to win the Democratic nomination the previous year before a few high-decibel missteps had derailed his candidacy, and his combative style and jagged partisanship made a lot of the powers-that-be in his party uneasy.[2]

You might think that Dean would use such a high profile appearance to put away donor concerns. But he had been elected to control the propaganda and fundraising arm of his party because its activists wanted someone in that position who wasn't afraid to rhetorically frag Republicans. In his appearance that Sunday, Dean demonstrated that he knew who had put him there and exactly what role they wanted him to play.

Dean hit on the theme of Republican corruption early in the interview. He started out by saying that President Bush's proposal for Social Security reform (the creation of individual accounts that are publicly regulated but privately invested in stocks, bonds, or other financial devices) was "kind of out there." The president, said Dean, "basically wants to turn over Social Security to the same kind of people who gave us Enron."

And so it continued. Then House Majority Leader Tom DeLay had been criticized several times by the House Ethics Committee and DeLay's reprehensible response, said Dean, had been to "get rid of the Ethics Committee, or render them inoperable." He argued that DeLay was "not an ethical person" and that the majority leader's lack of integrity should disqualify him from serving in congressional leadership.

Meet the Press host Tim Russert asked the DNC chairman about a few explosive remarks. Dean had said the majority leader "ought to go back to Houston, where he can serve his jail sentence down there courtesy of the Texas taxpayers." Russert wondered, "'Serve his jail sentence'? He—what's he been convicted of?" Dean's response began, "He hasn't been convicted yet," which led to an exchange of views, so to speak:

> **Russert:** You said in December of 2003 that we shouldn't prejudge Osama bin Laden. How can you sit here and have a different standard for Tom DeLay and prejudge him?

> **Dean:** To be honest with you, Tim, I don't think I'm prejudging him. . . .

He continued by saying that, in his nonprejudgment, there was "a reasonable chance that [DeLay] may end up in jail."

The interviewer refused to let that answer be the end of it. He asked if Dean's demonization of the Republican leadership might get in the way of a civilized and robust debate:

> **Russert:** Here's the Democratic National Committee Web site this morning. It is, in effect, a mug shot of Tom DeLay. You can see his height in the back with inches there, a serial number 18821. Is that appropriate, a mug shot?
>
> **Dean:** I don't think it's appropriate for Tom DeLay to be in Congress, Tim. I really don't. . . . I think he ought to at least step aside while this ethics investigation is going on. We didn't start this. Look, we're not going to stoop to the kind of divisiveness that the Republicans are doing and we're not going to stoop to the kind of abuse of power, but we are going to be tough as nails. This is a fight for the soul of America between the Republicans and Democrats.

Dean's pose was an interesting one. He repeatedly passed judgment while pretending not to be passing judgment, and he couched his condemnations in the rhetoric of self-defense. He brought up the subject of the majority leader in the first place and then said that the "point is not to bring up Tom DeLay, which I'm sure we will, and his ethics problems," when that was precisely the point. He wanted to rub Republicans' noses in the fact that the majority leader was under fire.

"TO ROOT OUT HYPOCRISY"

Russert continued to throw Dean's past statements back at him, forcing the new party boss to defend his words in front of a national audience. At one recent Democratic Party function, Dean had done an impression of talk radio king Rush Limbaugh snorting cocaine to mock Limbaugh's stay in a rehab clinic and ongoing legal problems over his addiction to painkillers.

The interviewer asked if it was appropriate to "mock somebody who's gone into therapy" to treat a drug addiction. The DNC chairman replied that the problem was "not that these folks have problems." Rather, he found it "galling to be lectured to about moral values by folks who have their own problems."

"Hypocrisy is a value that I think has been embraced by the Republican Party," he explained. "We get lectured by people all day long about moral values by people who have their own moral shortcomings. I don't think we ought to give a whole lot of lectures to people . . . and I don't think we ought to be lectured to by Republicans who have got all these problems themselves."

And again: "Everybody has ethical shortcomings. We ought not to lecture each other about our ethical shortcomings." This after he had said that Tom DeLay ought to be removed from office over his ethical shortcomings.

Dean pledged to use "whatever position I have to root out hypocrisy," by which he meant to tear Republicans down and build up the members of his own party as relative incorruptibles. In Dean's estimation, Republicans have a few pet hypocritical values and Democrats have their own "pretty strong moral values" that they ought to do a better job of fighting for.

He placed his list of values "in contradiction to the Republicans' [values]" and used each bulleted point to score a political one. Unlike the hypocritical Republicans, to paraphrase, we Democrats

- don't think children should go to bed hungry at night.

- wouldn't gamble away people's life savings in the stock market.

- have no desire to kick kids out of the public schools and shutter the doors.

- wouldn't treat Native Americans nearly so shoddily.

- believe universal publicly funded health care would be ideal.

At the end of this spiel, Dean announced that his own deeply held moral values were "offended by some of the things I hear on programs like *Rush Limbaugh*."

He used the platform to tell fellow Democrats their problem was that in the past they had been unwilling to "stand up early on and fight back against folks like [Limbaugh] who thought they were going to push us around and bully us, and we're not going to do it anymore. We don't have to put up with that."

STREET FIGHTING HAM

Now, think for a minute about the literal sense of some of Dean's words. "Root out hypocrisy," how exactly? Granted, "fight back" doesn't always mean literal fisticuffs, but isn't it sort of necessary for the back-and-forth of democracy that we have to at least pretend to put up with each other?

Not so much. In practice, republicanism is a much more vulgar, volatile, occasionally lethal medium than the civility-in-government types would like to admit. Remember, the third vice president of the United States shot our first secretary of the treasury dead in Weehawken, New Jersey, over an insult that the former secretary didn't even remember making.[3] Even Abraham Lincoln only narrowly averted a duel with broadswords, because his abnormally long arms gave him a tremendous advantage and forced a settlement.[4]

Remember, too, that in both cases the issue was not the public good but private grievance. It's possible, I suppose, to be too cynical about politics, but quite often public claims to high principle provide a fig leaf to cover over personal ambitions and rivalries. Many a critic of government corruption has become a champion of graft and privilege once in office, in part because the righteous critic of corruption is a role that voters expect our representatives to play before we're willing to give them the keys to the house.

Dr. Kris argues that what many people want from political leaders is the appearance of firm, unbending certainty. The best way to create that certainty in the minds of many is to lash out at the programs and missteps of political opponents in an overtly moralistic way. *They* are wrong about everything and *we* are right. Pushed to its logical limit (and Dean has been willing to push it that far): they are evil, we are good.

This all-or-nothing approach won't appeal to everyone, but it will appeal to many constituents who *want* to believe in something. It's a good way to excite the people who are already on your own side and to attract some of the voters who have doubts about the leadership of the ruling party, and it also serves as a way to further dim the aura of certainty of your opponents. Time that they are forced to spend fending off charges of mismanagement, corruption, or moral turpitude is time they can't spend party building or arguing for a positive vision.

That's how I understood Howard Dean's performance on *Meet the Press.* The former Vermont governor was trying to project an image of a middle-aged street fighting New Englander who wasn't going to stand for the rank hypocrisies of the GOP. His attacks were a way of going around the barn door to argue for his own virtue, and for the virtue of Democrats in general. He invited us to think of members of his own party as beyond corruption by attacking corruption.

The DNC chairman had attracted a devoted following in the presidential primaries with exactly this sort of message. He argued that President Bush had lied us into war and wrecked the country's finances with reckless tax cuts, and that it was time to muscle these unpleasant truths onto the public debate. If Bush was for it, Dean was (usually) agin' it, and so those people who opposed Bush latched on to Dean and held fast. The bond between the leader and his followers became an emotional one.

I helped edit a political Web site during the primary season and every time we published an article that criticized Dean or sounded skeptical about his chances of securing the Democratic nomination, the "Deaniacs" would rain down angry letters to the editor questioning our objectivity, our fairness, our sanity, and usually all three. Encouraged by their steadfast support, Dean soldiered on for far longer than any serious political analyst expected he would. He weathered loss after loss without conceding defeat.

On the day that Dean finally dropped out of the running, I was scheduled to observe a meeting of conservative activists in downtown Washington, D.C. I had purchased a novelty campaign-type button and wore it to the gathering as a gag without knowing quite how controversial it would become later in the day.

The button had a slogan in white lettering against a black backdrop. It was a play on the slacker phrase "Mean People Suck." It read, "Dean People Suck." That evening, when I took the Metro home to my Fairfax, Virginia, townhouse, my roommate Jim was along for the ride. Shortly after we got on, so did an early twenty-something-looking guy with dark hair, a backpack with several slogan patches, and an axe to grind.

The young Deaniac noticed the button and trained his eyes on me with what Jim described as "this very harsh, not particularly antiwar look." He continued to do double takes and shoot laser beams in my direction until he finally got off the train. It was clear as the bright blue sky that he wanted to start something, but Dean supporters had learned a hard lesson that day about the power of superior numbers, and two-on-one apparently were not his kind of odds. So Dean's statement, "We don't have to put up with that [i.e., nonviolent criticism]," could be taken as a fairly menacing boast.

THE WRIGHT STUFF

In fairness, Howard Dean may be a great example of our modern obsession with hypocrisy, but he is far from unique. And he's not completely nuts to think charges of corruption could bring his party back to power. By laying into alleged ethical lapses of Republicans, Dean was simply trying to replicate a style of politics that had been perfected most recently by Newt Gingrich.

Gingrich is a famously combative Republican who was elected to the House of Representatives from Georgia in 1978. He worked his way up the chain of command of his own party by the force of his own ambition and intellect, and with political instincts that were just a little bit ahead of their time.

The Georgia congressman took advantage of the fact that C-SPAN was covering the House at all times to speak to viewers. He delivered impassioned speeches against the Democrats when the House wasn't conducting regular business. The Democratic leadership was so incensed by this that they ordered the cable channel to pan the chamber every so often, to show viewers that Gingrich was speaking to an empty House.[5]

Early on, Gingrich developed a talent for mucking about in House ethics scandals. He called for the expulsion of Congressmen Dan Crane and Gerry Studds when it came out that they'd had sex with underage congressional pages, and the whole House voted to formally reprimand both men.[6] In 1987, he lodged the ethics complaint against Speaker of the House Jim Wright that eventually led Wright to resign from Congress.

As the second in command of the House Republicans, Gingrich led a minirevolt in 1990 against the first President Bush when Bush gave in to the Democrats' demand to raise taxes to help reduce the size of the deficit. He very publicly spoke out against the budget, calling it a "recession-increasing, job-killing, tax-increasing, and deficit-increasing package."[7]

Freed from the obligation to defend George H. W. Bush's policies and pitfalls, Republicans managed to pick up nine seats in the House in 1992 and to stage a historic victory two years later. In 1994 the GOP took fifty-four new seats in the House and eight in the Senate, gaining control of both bodies for the first time since before *Mister Ed* went off the air.

AN ALMOST PERFECT STORM

A big reason for the Republicans' victory was the ethical cloud that followed Democrats wherever they went and hurled thunderbolts at them every time they opened their mouths. Granted, President Bill Clinton's tendency to tell audiences what he thought they wanted to hear harmed the credibility of his party. And charges that First Lady Hillary Clinton wanted to ram a Canadian-style single-payer overhaul of our health care system through Congress didn't help. But a number of scandals also came together to blow away the old regime.

The first major scandal was the House Bank Scandal, nicknamed Rubbergate for the thousands of bounced checks that congressmen had written to the House Bank, a federally subsidized private "bank" for our House members to deposit and draw on their payroll checks. In late September 1991, the congressional newspaper *Roll Call* broke the story that 134 representatives had bounced checks for $1,000 or more in one year alone.[8]

Looking back on the scandal, *Roll Call* editors wrote, "everything that Congress did [suddenly] fell under the microscope," including such privileges as "getting parking tickets fixed, dining credit cards and an ambulance for Members [of Congress] only."[9] The House Bank was abolished before year's end, but the matter wasn't finished.

Faced with the fact that over 350 current and past members had bounced checks totaling millions of dollars, the House Ethics Committee decided to release a list of a few dozen of the most flagrant violators in early '92. The revelations smashed the normal incumbent advantages to pieces and led to a wave of retirements, resignations, and lost races over the next few election cycles.

The House Bank scandal opened the door to other scandals as well. Reporters kept digging into banking records, furiously filing Freedom of Information Act requests, and generally sniffing out other potential ethical violations or broken laws.

In July 1993, on the floor of the House, New York Congressman Bill Paxon said of one scandal that it "represents in microcosm all that is wrong with this House, forty years of one-party control, doors closed to public scrutiny, and putting personal interest above the public interest."[10] The rhetoric could have been applied to any number of ethical tremors, but this case was the House Post Office scandal. Congressmen had been using the House Post office to trade stamps and postal vouchers in for mad money.

And so it went. In 1994, powerful Ways and Means Committee Chairman Dan Rostenkowski resigned from the House after he was indicted for mail fraud, and for enriching himself by raiding his own campaign funds (he would eventually plead guilty and serve fifteen months in prison). In any other year, this might have been seen as an isolated incident of corruption, but instead it was cast as something larger and more menacing.

Gingrich and company used every embarrassing revelation to build an indictment. They argued that Democrats were both wrong and corrupt, and that they needed to go. The dilemma that they faced was the fact that many of these scandals implicated Republicans as well, though to a lesser extent than the Democrats.

The congressional GOP had to do something to get beyond the idea that "everybody does it." They had, in other words, to find some way to make voters believe in them. And so Newt Gingrich stepped forward with his masterstroke and his John Hancock.

CONTRACT NEGOTIATIONS

Six weeks before the election, the GOP rolled out its big gun, a piece of paper signed by all but two House Republicans and all of the candidates for the lower house. It was a plan of action for a new Republican House. Newspapers and cable news covered it but weren't quite sure what to make of it.

The Contract With America, as the document was called, was really two documents stitched together. It was a pledge to bring to the floor of the House ten proposals that addressed poll-tested popular policy reforms, including ordering that U.S. troops not serve under United Nations command, imposing term limits, and capping punitive damages on lawsuits. It was also something altogether more ingenious.

The preamble pledged that, if elected, an incoming Republican majority would act "not just to change [the House's] policies, but even more important, to restore the bonds of trust between the people and their elected representatives."[11]

The righteous tone continued down the page. The document was issued during "this era of official evasion and posturing" and was pitched against the spirit of the age. The signatories of the Contract were proposing a "detailed agenda for national renewal, a written commitment with no fine print." You could take this one to the bank and it would not come back marked "insufficient funds" like the House Bank checks.

The House Republicans and candidates for office promised to "restore accountability to Congress. To end its cycle of scandal and disgrace. To make us all proud again of the way free people govern themselves." Theirs would be a *do something* Congress, and then some. They would vote on all ten Contract items within the first hundred days.

Before the Contract began to spell the issues out, it committed the signers to eight reforms that they would enact on the first *day* of the new session to begin the hard job of "restoring the faith and trust of the American people in their government." To wit:

FIRST, require all laws that apply to the rest of the country also apply equally to the Congress;

SECOND, select a major, independent auditing firm to conduct a comprehensive audit of Congress for waste, fraud or abuse;

THIRD, cut the number of House committees, and cut committee staff by one-third;

FOURTH, limit the terms of all committee chairs;

FIFTH, ban the casting of proxy votes in committee;

SIXTH, require committee meetings to be open to the public;

SEVENTH, require a three-fifths majority vote to pass a tax increase;

EIGHTH, guarantee an honest accounting of our Federal Budget by implementing zero base-line budgeting.[12]

The document sounded many small government notes, and it would be foolish to discount the real anger with the overreaches of government. But the tune was all about vice and virtue, corruption and incorruption, horns and halos. It helped to focus the press and Republicans on those themes that determined the outcome of the election.

Republicans convinced enough voters to trust them to tip the balance in their favor. They created that trust by calling the Democrats a bunch of crooks, cheats, liars, and hypocrites. And they were soon to discover that payback isn't pretty.

"NEWT! NEWT! NEWT!"

On November 9, 1994, Gingrich entered his election head-quarters in Georgia's sixth district to cries of "Newt! Newt! Newt!" and "Speaker! Speaker! Speaker!" He had barnstormed the country in support of Republican candidates for Congress, laying into the shortcomings and scandals of Democrats in more than one hundred districts, and speaking in favor of the virtues of Republican rule.

In fact, Democrats had tried to make him into an election issue. A vote for *Candidate X* was a vote for *Newt Gingrich* to lead the House of Representatives, and who wanted that?

But voters preferred this relative unknown to the devil that they knew all too well. And now, on election night, Gingrich had done the unthinkable. He had engineered a complete transfer of power from the Democrats to the Grand Old Party, shifting the natural center of government in one campaign.

Gingrich quieted the crowd and said a few words, but it was hard to contain the excitement. There was no question but that this man would be elected the next speaker of the House, and it appeared that he was genuinely interested in changing the rancorous way that business was done in D.C.

The future Speaker promised to be not just fair but "dramatically more fair than the Democrats have been in my lifetime." Republicans and all men of goodwill would work to "build together a great majority to do good things for America."

In response to some anti-Clinton catcalls from supporters, he quoted Britain's great wartime Prime Minister Winston Churchill for advice about what to do next. "In battle courageous, in defeat defiant, and in victory magnanimous," Gingrich cautioned them.

There would be some investigations into the irregularities of the Clinton administration, he promised, but there would be no witch hunts, and political disagreements didn't have to be quite so nasty in the future. Instead, he hoped that the president would sit down with GOP leaders and try to find some common ground on items from the Contract With America, and that they collectively could work to restore the trust of the American people in their government.

The AP reporter wrote that Gingrich "was as gracious in victory as he had been pugnacious in his drive to end Democratic domination of the House."[13] And the victorious politician indicated that he understood that barbarians and statesmen must behave differently.

"I don't think that Newt Gingrich the Republican whip is the same behavior pattern in terms of style and speeches and aggression that you'd want to have in the Speaker of the House," he explained.

But issues of hypocrisy and integrity weren't about to go away just because the Republicans had retaken Congress. To rip the words of another British prime minister wildly out of context and put them to better use: "A Conservative government is an organized hypocrisy."[14] Any time you have to balance deeply held principles against the demands of office, you are going to have contradictions and compromises. And the closer people look, the more problems they are likely to notice.

In Gingrich's case, the scrutiny was severe. Over the next few years, David Bonior, a Michigan congressman and the House

Democratic whip, would hound Gingrich more fiercely than Gingrich had ever dogged Democrats. Bonior and colleagues filed scores of ethics complaints against Speaker Gingrich for things ranging from a book deal to the funding of a college course that Gingrich taught in his spare time.

Though he was never formally censured by the Ethics Committee, Gingrich did have to pay a whopping fine, euphemistically described as a "cost assessment." He was forced to cough up $300,000 for having unintentionally misled members of the committee about a matter that is so arcane it would make your head spin (well, it made *my* head spin).[15]

And Gingrich lasted only four years as speaker. He was deposed by members of the party that he had brought to power because they thought he had become a liability. Part of his liability came from the bad taste that the ethics investigations had left in voters' mouths.

ETHICS, SCHMETHICS

Some conservatives responded to Bonior's agitation by urging the Ethics Committee to look into the minority whip's own alleged misuse of staff for his own private business. And the ethical dog would have kept chasing after its own tail if both parties of Congress had not voted to curtail the power of the Ethics Committee.

But here is a question: Why does the House even *have* an Ethics Committee? What purpose does it serve? We already have people to sniff out scandals and raise hell. They're called reporters, government watchdog groups, and political rivals. And if the infractions rise to the level of criminality, we have prosecutors whose careers are rarely harmed by going after sitting congressmen. As far as judging the ethical conduct of individual House members is concerned, we have people for that too. They're called voters.

If your answer to the Ethics Committee question is "to keep congressmen honest," then I respectfully ask that you think again. In extraordinary circumstances, Congress need not even accept the choice of the voters as binding. Thoroughly scandalous members occasionally are kicked out.

In 2002, Ohio's toupeed wonder James Traficant was expelled from the House after he was convicted of taking bribes, racketeering, cheating on his taxes, and using public employees for his own private projects. Only the lame duck Representative Gary Condit, who had lost his own party's nomination after an incident involving a missing, murdered intern came to light, voted against Traficant's removal. And thus the judgment of the seventeenth district of Ohio was set aside.

But barring special, awful circumstances, why shouldn't ethical determinations be up to the voters? In the past, the House Ethics Committee often indulged an impulse that was badly misguided. The committee members were concerned not just with whether members have behaved lawfully but also whether their actions had the "appearance of impropriety."

That unfortunate focus drags Congress into the murky area of "appearance ethics," a concern not so much with the truth of things as with how they look at a glance, to the most ill-informed angry outsider. Rules that are passed with those assumptions in mind are not likely to be workable ones.

Lawyer Peter Morgan and University of Tennessee law professor Glenn Reynolds (now of Instapundit.com fame) examined the effect of appearance ethics in a little-noticed book that was published in 1997, *The Appearance of Impropriety*. The authors framed the spread of appearance ethics over the last few decades as "ultimately, a story of institutional breakdown and failure to take moral responsibility—a story of the substitution of appearances for substance, of technicalities for judgment, of opportunism for self-discipline."[16]

"Opportunism" was a very good word. The history of House ethics allegations is a history of ambition concealed as crusading indignation. And the rulings of the Ethics Committee often helped to shift blame and mislead voters rather than make the House more ethical.

Take even the most obvious of all political scandals, the House Bank Scandal. The House Bank was not a bank as most people would think of it. The records were not kept on computer, and it often took weeks for the bank to post deposits or determine that a congressman had overdrawn his account. Congressmen were not issued regular statements. The Bank rarely flagged overdrafts.

In fact, "overdraw" is probably a misleading term. There was an informal rule that congressmen could take out more money as long as the amount didn't exceed their next paycheck. For many congressmen, an overdraft was really an advance on guaranteed future earnings. That was certainly a nice perk, and prone to abuse, but it seems, in hindsight, a petty reason to send dozens of congressional careers down in flames. Some congressmen did defraud the House Bank but they were in the minority, and the criteria that the House Ethics Committee used to determine the flagrant violators didn't take into account whether the money was ever paid back.

That's right, the committee that was devoted to *ethics* refused to distinguish between thieves and stragglers. If Tom DeLay had gotten rid of it like Howard Dean half-charged, he might have done the country a great favor.

CLINTON AND OTHER FALLACIES

One huge problem with arguments about ethics is the way that leaders make a play for public sympathy by proposing stricter rules. This strategy touched the outer reaches of absurdity when President Clinton responded to credible charges that he broke campaign finance laws during his reelection campaign by boasting that, unlike Republicans, *he* favored campaign finance reform legislation.

That didn't make any sense—I broke the rules but I favor stricter rules, so *I* get a pass?—but our forty-second president benefited from what we might call the Clinton Fallacy on more than one occasion. In another oft-noted example, prominent feminists very publicly gave him a pass on allegations of bad behavior toward women because he had toughened up sexual harassment laws and never met an antiabortion bill he couldn't veto.

It was odd and troubling to see Democratic flacks on cable networks using the "but we're for reform" argument with a straight face, and to find that those arguments had been taken seriously when you talked to the guy on the street. The Clinton Fallacy was a way of declaring their own virtue that resonated with Democrat-leaning voters. It gave those voters something to believe in, a way to swat off objections to the president's behavior. And it worked.

It worked because those crucial voters feared the alternative—and for another reason as well. To his list of reasons why otherwise intelligent people are fooled by hypocrites, Dr. Kris said that "strong desires must be considered as coconspirators at least."[17] Clinton supporters didn't *want* the allegations to be true, and so reached for any justification they could find. Stop me if you've heard this one:

> *Everybody does it.*
>
> *Unlike my opponent, I support campaign finance reform.*
>
> *There's a vast right-wing conspiracy.*
>
> *All those hundreds of people who slept in the Lincoln bedroom were personal friends of the president.*

These sorts of defenses left critics of Clinton dumbfounded and spitting mad. How could people not see through such obvious evasions? What was wrong with them? Why, the lies and the hypocrisy were so thick that you could cut them with a knife. How could people not see that? Losing presidential candidate Bob Dole wondered, "Where is the outrage?" That was only a slightly more polite way of asking, "What the hell is wrong with you people?"

Clinton is a great example of appearance ethics gone wild, but this isn't a particularly conservative or a liberal thing. Republicans and Democrats are regularly condemned for their alleged hypocrisies by their opposite numbers. And the people yelling "hypocrisy!" are often right. Politicians do often violate their ideals for their own gain, or cynically profess ideals that they don't actually hold to make people think better of them. But politicians are hardly unique in that respect.

What critics left and right do not understand is the enduring value of hypocrisy. They see it as something wicked that should be "rooted out" and attempt to do so with ever more rules, with public disapproval, and with an increased and unwarranted scrutiny of how things appear. All the attempts to stamp out hypocrisy only change its face.

Today's critic of hypocrisy is tomorrow's example of the need to throw the bums out because hypocrisy is not an aberration but a fairly recurrent feature of the human condition. We want and need others to think well of us.

The image that we project to the outside world through word and deed is often a caricature of what we are like after the curtain has gone down. In Clinton's case, advisor Dick Morris explained the difference between the man's behavior in public and in private with one deft rhetorical stroke. We had Saturday Night Bill, who was a bit of a scoundrel and a troublemaker. And then it was time for sermons and soda water.[18] Sunday Morning Bill carried a huge Bible under his arm, felt your pain, and railed against the scandals and corruption of the first Bush administration. Clinton succeeded, as many politicians have succeeded, by puffing up his own virtue and damning his opponents' vices.

Clinton made people want to believe in him, against considerable evidence. That belief became his sword and his shield.

SCANTILY CLAD HYPOCRISIES

Politics is a good place to start looking at hypocrisy because the smoke-filled back rooms are often bugged and the private rarely stays private. Politics is useful to observe because it has become the modern equivalent of ancient Greek drama. The ambition is scantily clad, the partisan struggles are predictable, the sanctimony is well-rehearsed, and we recognize many of the players on stage as they bring the same old scripts to life.

Washington, D.C., manages to be both packed to the rafters with hypocrites and yet constantly scandalized at their hypocrisy. The conventional wisdom—the talking points that are recycled over and over again on television and in print by journalists and party hacks—is our own Greek chorus of woe, clucking over ethics violations, drawing out the contradictions, and heralding doom for more failed reformers.

The spectacle can be entertaining or maddening, depending on your preference, but it's not unique. Nor is it surprising unless we're talking about the shock of recognition. Drama works because it connects with our own experience, and we experience hypocrisy all the time.

In trying to get a better handle on hypocrisy, I searched out a man who knew a great deal about the subject. He told me a story. . . .

3

DO AS I DON'T

Well, that's hypocrisy, of course.

ALEKSANDR SOLZHENITSYN

James Spiegel remembers well "my earliest and most vivid memory of hypocrisy."[1] It was during the summer of his thirteenth year. A neighbor who lived across the street from the Spiegel residence in the city of Jackson, Mississippi, hired the young teenager, along with a friend, to mow and edge the man's lawn. The neighbor was going away for the weekend, but he agreed to pay them $25 when he returned.

Spiegel and his buddy worked much of the day into the fading of Saturday evening, cutting and edging and bagging the grass clippings. It was a large lawn and they still weren't quite done by dusk. They returned Sunday morning and finished up as promised.

On Monday, they went to collect the money, and one of the boys let it slip that it had taken two days to get the job done. Spiegel admits that they were probably hoping for a tip, but he didn't expect the exchange that followed.

"Two days?" the man said. "You mean to tell me that you mowed my lawn on Sunday?"

They nodded.

"Well, boys, I don't allow work to be done at my house on Sundays. I can't pay you."

The neighbor dug into his pants pockets for some loose change and gave them about $2. He explained, "I'm doing this out of the kindness of my heart."

The boys didn't know quite what to say, so they said nothing and sulked back to Spiegel's house. Jim told his father what had just happened. His old man exploded.

"Hypocrites! Lousy hypocrites! They smile so sweetly and look so righteous at church, but in the real world they're nothing but swindlers and cheats."

Spiegel told me when I talked to him in October of 2005 that was the first time that he'd heard the word *hypocrite* and added, "It was the first time I heard some other words as well." But it was far from the last time he'd hear his father sound off on the subject.

In fact, he said, the topic became a well-worn father-son theme. Spiegel, Sr. complained loudly about the two-facedness and duplicity of moralists in general and religious types in particular, who could preach it out but couldn't—or wouldn't—practice it.

He then used incidents of hypocrisy to set up a contrast. Sure, I have problems, he would freely admit, but then I don't pretend to be a font of virtue. "At least," he would say, "at least I am not a hypocrite."

It's easy to understand why Spiegel's father would revile such double-dealing behavior. "'Hypocrite' is an epithet, never a term of praise and for good reason," says Duke philosopher and political scientist Ruth Grant. "When an old woman is persuaded to 'invest' her life savings in a phony pension fund we are considerably more outraged than when she loses it all in an ordinary robbery."[2] The hypocrisy adds insult to loss.

Given Spiegel's experience with hypocrisy, you might expect that he followed in his father's lead, that he cursed those hypocrites and had nothing to do with them. No reasonable person could have blamed him for it. But instead he did something far more interesting.

IN THIS CORNER

These days James Spiegel is Professor Spiegel. He teaches philosophy at Taylor University, a medium-sized liberal arts college in Indiana, with campuses in Upland and Fort Wayne, that has been around since before the Civil War. The school is non-denominational and vaguely evangelical, named for the Methodist Bishop William Taylor.

Spiegel landed on the Upland campus twelve years ago, one year out of his Ph.D. program and coming off a stint at Minnesota State University as a fill-in for a professor on sabbatical. The job market for new doctors of philosophy, he told me, was underheated at the time, and the Indiana school seemed like it might be a decent fit. But as Spiegel's reputation has grown over the last dozen years, he has stayed put. I wanted to know why.

Spiegel explained that he enjoys the job and the general

intellectual climate at the university: goodness, truth, beauty, *and* a regular paycheck. Granted, any class will have "a few bad eggs but, you know, particularly my philosophy majors are committed to the life of learning," he said. Eager, serious students, combined with supportive faculty, make it "a good situation."

That was a rough synonym for a sweet deal. Taylor has given him plenty of room to pursue his interests. To wit, he produces music in his own recording studio at his home in nearby Fairmount. Spiegel has cut a few solo albums, and lately he's taken to recording and performing as part of the blues-rock band, The Joneses.

Allowing Spiegel to keep up with the Joneses had paid off for Taylor because his private interests are bundled together with his professional ones. He was invited to contribute essays to publisher Open Court's philosophy and pop culture titles *Bob Dylan and Philosophy* and *The Beatles and Philosophy*, and he's published widely on the intersection of film and thought. He explained, "Where philosophy and the arts meet, I am interested."

Spiegel uses his professorial freedom to great effect. Through his articles, tutorials, and classes, he regularly explores modes of thinking that catch his fancy. These range from the morality of terrorism to the writings of the eighteenth-century philosopher Bishop George Berkeley (in his solo music act, Spiegel stole the stage name Philonous from a character in one of Berkeley's dialogues) to the importance of "the virtues," as he shorthands them.

The thing about this adopted-Hoosier professor that caught my attention was a project he formally undertook in 1996. Spiegel released the first installment three years later with

Hypocrisy: Moral Fraud and Other Vices. It's not a long book, but it is, so far as I could tell, the first of its kind. It's a hypocrisy primer that walks readers through the history and workings of the idea.

Most writing about hypocrisy is either short and polemical or lengthy, highly technical, and limited in focus. In his first contribution to the study of self-contradiction, Professor Spiegel managed to find a better way. He wrote something that was not simple but no more complicated than necessary, and broad enough to be useful.

The beginning of this project, Spiegel told me, was in his father's reaction to the crooked religious neighbor. In those two figures, he observed two distinctly different *types* of people, who were really not so different.

Think of it as a boxing match. In one corner, you had a bona fide hypocrite using "sham righteousness" to justify his non-payment, and pay himself a compliment to boot. And back against the ropes at the other end of the ring, you had the classic antihypocrite, venting his rage not so much at the actor or the action but on an entire class of people—moralists, God fearers, churchgoers—and then using that palpable disgust to, well, to pay himself a compliment, and to rationalize his own behavior. And when the bell sounded, they didn't bother to lay a glove on each other. They didn't even come out of their corners.

Spiegel's response to this age-old conflict was philosophical, and complicated. He decided to disagree with both the hypocrite and the antihypocrite, and to cast about for an alternative.

"From then on I had a certain sensitivity to the hypocrisy of anyone who pretends to maintain high moral standards," he said.

Spiegel also noticed, in popular culture and in his dealings with others, how people would use hypocrisy as a way of dismissing concerns about morality and religion, which he considered "pretty flimsy" reasoning.

Spiegel's search for better reasoning led him to write *the* book on hypocrisy (before this one). I guessed that this would make him both a good guide to the subject and an ideal whetstone to try out a few ideas. So, fairly early into our interview, I asked him, "Dr. Spiegel, are you a hypocrite?"

The first word out of his mouth was "uh." The second was "well." The third was "um." He then rallied and described himself as a "morally serious person." I believe him.

"I KNOW IT WHEN I SEE IT"

Spiegel's hesitation was telling. It spoke of the difficulty in defining hypocrisy and applying that judgment to our lives. Supreme Court Justice Potter Stewart once said of pornography, "I know it when I see it," but that's not always true with hypocrisy.[3] As with drug tests, there is the serious problem of "false positives." Many people saw hypocrisy in the Bill Bennett gambling incident, but I argue that there was none. Who's right?

The problem is that hypocrisy involves a kind of deception that can be hard to spot. The simplest definition that Spiegel could offer was "a certain kind of inconsistency that always involves behavior and sometimes involves one's beliefs or spoken words." Which is clear as mud.

It's a little easier to get at a working definition if you throw passion into the mix. Why, I asked, is hypocrisy nearly universally condemned? What's the big deal?

"I think because it's a double vice," Spiegel said. "It involves not just the indiscretion that one's covering up but also the indiscretion of the deception. Also, we despise the fact that hypocrites justify themselves and often profit by their deception, so there's a deep injustice there."

The "double vice" approach to hypocrisy was introduced by Thomas Aquinas, an Italian Dominican friar and theologian born in the thirteenth century. The dumb ox, as Aquinas was unfortunately nicknamed, said the problem with hypocrites is that they do bad things and then, in effect, lie about them by acting like moral, upstanding citizens.

Hypocrites often use their misgotten reputation for honesty or piety to fend off legitimate grievances. To get a picture of what this looks like in practice, you need think no further than two teenage boys, standing on their neighbor's porch, mouths agape, not knowing quite how to respond to the man's refusal to pay what he owes, wrapped as it is in the language of piety and pity (e.g., "out of the kindness of my heart").

Spiegel follows Aquinas's thinking on many of hypocrisy's finer distinctions. He agrees, for instance, that some people who we might be tempted to call hypocrites should not be thought of in quite that way. Some people suffer from *akrasia*, or moral weakness, rather than from full-blown hypocrisy.

Two young sweethearts may believe in saving it until marriage but make it to second base and keep right on going. Or a teenage girl may know that shoplifting is wrong but sees a red leather purse that she's just got to have, but that she hasn't got the money for.

These things may look and feel an awful lot like hypocrisy. After all, they involve contradicting one's stated ideals. But according to Spiegel and Aquinas, they likely are not.

NOT THAT INNOCENT

"What is missing in moral weakness," the Taylor professor explained, "is the sham righteousness that hypocrisy involves. We don't call Darryl Strawberry or Britney Spears a fraud because of their behavior because they never claim to be righteous. But a Jimmy Swaggart or a Rafael Palmeiro, that's a different story."

However, one of Spiegel's examples demonstrates just how hard it can be to distinguish between contradictions that result from hypocrisy and contradictions borne of moral weakness: the case of Britney Spears. Spears is a dancer and pop singer who joined the cast of the television show *The Mickey Mouse Club* at the tender age of eleven, and released her first hit single when she was seventeen.

Spears was advertised as a fairly conventional girl from a Baptist family, and her early public actions didn't veer too far from the sales pitch. Her breakout music video featured the young starlet dancing with a troupe in Catholic schoolgirl uniforms, skirts cut to roughly regulation length. The first album cover is a picture of Spears against a light pink background, looking like a normal, slightly awkward teenage girl: loose-fitting red blouse over a white shirt, winning smile, no navel showing. Also, she let it be known that she didn't believe in sex before marriage.[4]

This retro image helped to turn Spears into an unprecedented

success. The former Mouseketeer built an audience of adoring, mostly younger teenage girls, in part by not freaking out their parents, who would pay for and often chaperone the teenyboppers to concerts. The kids could sell her as a modern blonde version of Annette Funicello, and how do you argue with that? Not very effectively, apparently. Spears's first album sold over 14 million copies in the United States alone.

It's unlikely that the girl I just described is the same one that popped into your head when you heard the name "Britney Spears." There is a reason for that. Between her debut album in 1999 and her present turn as a newly married mother trying to reinvent herself, Spears's public image shifted along with her private behavior.

Though Spears repeatedly denied rumors that she and her boyfriend, N*SYNC singer Justin Timberlake, were having sex, she eventually admitted the affair. On stage, the outfits grew skimpier and the lyrics lustier. Some music videos simulated S&M fantasies, others cast her as an erotic dancer. At the MTV 2003 Music Awards, she traded a *faux* lesbian French kiss with Madonna. She made headlines again in 2004 when she impulsively tied the knot with a childhood friend during a visit to the Las Vegas strip, and then quickly annulled the marriage.

Spears's changing behavior has led to charges of hypocrisy, and worse. When I reported on the Conservative Political Action Committee convention of activists in Crystal City, Virginia, in early 2004, one booth that promoted family values issues had a troll toss game. People were invited to heft beanbags at several toy trolls that held up signs including "gay marriage" and, yes, "Britney Spears."

Critics say that she did her part to sex up adolescent teenage girls, and that some of her lyrics have disturbing bondage undercurrents. At a domestic violence conference in 2003, Kendel Ehrlich, first lady of the state of Maryland, quipped that she would like to "shoot Britney Spears."[5]

Professor Spiegel believes that we are able to tell the difference between hypocrisy and moral weakness by "contextual clues" over time. "It's not often when someone's deep sham gets uncovered," he said, "but then it becomes very clear that this person wasn't just morally weak. There was a deception here." However, in the Britney Spears case the evidence is inconclusive and likely always to be so, and I think what is true of her is true of many.

It is undeniably true that Spears owes a large part of her success to her early wholesome image. It allowed her to build up an audience and that audience made her known in the larger world of musicians and celebrities. She definitely profited from this deception, if there was one.

Inquiring minds may want to know: Was this singer the person she represented herself as at the start of her solo career: a young, relatively innocent performer of limited vision but boundless enthusiasm? Or was she something else, something more calculating and sinister, like the diabolical figure some of her critics have railed against? Did she get carried away in the navel-raising currents of Hollywood culture and the advice of her manager, or was she a one-woman tsunami?

The Spears case also raises the "people change" issue. Early on, she was more explicitly moralistic, now much less so. Surely there's some kind of statute of limitations on these things. Most

of us are not what we once were, for good or for ill. And yet, for all her skimp and skin, Spears publicly turned down an offer from *Playboy* to pose nude for $1 million. It wouldn't have been much more than she's already shown us, but I guess there was a line to be drawn somewhere, and she drew it.

"IT'S NOT A LIE IF YOU BELIEVE IT"

Most of us lump moral weakness and hypocrisy together as plain-vanilla hypocrisy because we find it useful to do so, at least when we are considering the behavior of others. It's more practical to point out the contradiction between creed and deed than to puzzle over the reason for that contradiction. Knowing hypocrisy would be a mysterious, almost occult activity if we had to sift it too finely.

But what of ourselves? When I asked Spiegel why so few books have been written about hypocrisy, he guessed that it was because the subject is "deceivingly complex." From a distance, it appears simple, but the closer you get to it, the more you feel like running away screaming. And by far the most terrifying part of the taxonomy of hypocrisy is self-deception.

"I ended up neck deep in journal articles just in psychology" to sort through the issue of self-deception, Spiegel explained. "The question of whether hypocrisy does or does not involve self-deception is itself a book length, or multivolume-worth, kind of inquiry. And whole books have been written on self-deception, what it is, even if it's real."

Spiegel waded through the arguments about the "if" and the "how" of self-deception and came up for air on the other side. He decided that self-deception does occur. It involves both cognition (knowledge) and volition (the will). Self-deception influences our actions at one end and determines how we think about those actions on the other end. And just because someone is self-deceived doesn't mean he's not a hypocrite.

The professor argues that people who are self-deceived can be hypocrites because, at some level, you have to know that a thing is true in order to misrepresent it, even to misrepresent it to yourself. That great dissembling *Seinfeld* character, George Costanza, once offered his own expert advice on how to beat a polygraph test: "Jerry, just remember, it's not a lie if you believe it."[6]

Self-deceptive hypocrisy is a many-splendored thing. The most famous example from politics is best expressed in the phrase "plausible deniability." That is, someone in a position of power gives vague assent to unsavory or illegal actions undertaken by his underlings or other agents, and does not want to know the details. He can then claim, in public or in a court of law, that he had no idea, really, if the actions are ever uncovered. "No idea" is a stretch, but it's true that he didn't know much. That's part of the deception.

What's more, many of our normal activities are fraught with hypocrisy of the self-deceptive variety. Psychologists must marvel at their patients' ability to rationalize almost any behavior as being acceptable or excusable, given one's goals or extenuating circumstances. There is an overpowering urge to think of ourselves as "okay" or "not so bad," and we don't like to be told otherwise.

We often employ our own mental triangulation in order to get there. "I'm not as rich as Bill Gates or my neighbor down the street but at least I'm not on welfare." Or: "I shouldn't swear this much but have you heard the kids these days?" More to the point: "I may not be the world's best (fill in the blank) but at least I am not a hypocrite." People who make this last claim are very often being hypocritical about hypocrisy.

But not all forms of deception are hypocritical. Spiegel offered the example of moral irony, the "practice of appearing less virtuous than you are," often in order to make a point. The Athenian gadfly Socrates was a great moral ironist. He publicly regarded himself as "truly ignorant and not wise but in fact it was because he saw the limits of his own understanding that he was the wisest [man] in all of Athens and maybe one of the wisest [men] that ever lived."

With moral irony, said Spiegel, "there's a lack of a match, again between the reality and the presentation. But we don't consider that bad." However, we might consider it annoying. The men of ancient Athens put the philosopher through a show trial and tried to exile him. When that didn't work, they sentenced him to death. And then there's that old rabbinic jab directed at false humility: "Who are you to be so humble?"

Spiegel also brought up a kind of behavior that most people take for granted: "There's a certain commonality that some kinds of hypocrisy have with, of all things, manners. Or public decency," he explained. "We wear our best face for others. Even a very trivial thing, someone asks you on the elevator how you're doing and you say, 'Fine.' Actually you're not fine. You've got a bad toothache and your dog's at the vet. But these are things we do just to keep a kind of social order."

The reason that we don't consider manners to be hypocritical is what some wag might label the Reverse George Costanza Exception: it's not a lie if everyone knows it to be false.

HOW TO BE BAD

When I asked the professor if hypocrisy is always bad, he replied that it is, indeed, wicked. But his initial answer ("I think hypocrisy is always bad") proved to be only the first layer of the onion. The further we got to the core, the more he started to question his own assumption.

He admits that hypocrisy can produce the occasional good effect, or "positive externality." The term comes from the field of economics. An externality is a cost or a benefit that someone other than the person making the economic decision either pays or reaps.

If I buy an electric guitar, a drum kit, and amplification equipment, my neighbors may experience "negative externalities" at three in the morning. If I hail from a large family and over-order at a restaurant, it's likely that one of my siblings will experience a "positive externality" the next time he opens the refrigerator.

The externality argument bears some resemblance to a quip that contrarians have been using to defend hypocrisy for hundreds of years. Seventeenth-century French noble François De La Rochefoucauld opined that hypocrisy is the "tribute that vice pays to virtue."[7] But what is the price that virtue exacts? How, exactly, does hypocrisy force vice to reach for its wallet?

In one of *Hypocrisy's* more insightful passages, Spiegel

contemplates the "bright side to this moral blight." He spells out a few of the would-be benefits of self-contradiction. One, the "pretentious hypocrite" might have an overall "positive effect by modeling certain virtues." Two, hypocrites may inspire others to do good with their words, even if their deeds are not admirable. People who "take morality seriously" may be "duped by the moral impostors among us" to go out and do the right thing. Spiegel allows that "to this extent the effects of hypocrisy are beneficial."

But what happens if the hypocrite is found out, thus putting the lie to his fraudulent actions and throwing his preachments into question? Spiegel still sees a third, indirect benefit to hypocrisy. It's an insight that should earn him some kind of Evil Pollyanna Award. He points to the "outrage public hypocrisies inspire." The worked-up reactions may lead to "deeper moral introspection for the rest of us," or it might just force us to alter our behavior "to save ourselves the embarrassment of public ridicule."

"Deeper moral introspection" was the lightly trod path that led the Taylor professor to the next installment of his study of deception. *How to Be Good in a World Gone Bad* was the self-helpful title of his second book. Its subject is the virtues: their history, their importance, and how to practice them.

Spiegel acknowledges that the work was itself a kind of positive externality of his study of hypocrisy. Some may say that "the light reveals the darkness," but, you see, "sometimes the darkness reveals the light. It was depressing in a lot of ways to think so much about vice and I just needed relief. But one of the things I found, specifically, in looking at hypocrisy as well as moral weakness is the importance of sincerity and humility as virtues."

ONIONS HAVE LAYERS

I let the professor finish his answer, but it was tough to resist blurting out a question. I'd read what he had to say about hypocrisy, lingered over it, digested it. And it seemed to me there was a disconnect in how most of us think about hypocrisy.

Spiegel had said that hypocrisy is always bad, and then qualified this judgment so that it applied only to "moral hypocrisy." Granted, hypocrisy can have some good effects, but for philosophers and moralists, including Spiegel, the rightness of a thing is not supposed to be decided only by its effects. In the sixteenth century, Niccolo Machiavelli, a sometimes civil servant from the Italian city-state of Florence, wrote in a privately circulated manuscript that lasting and peaceful ends would justify brutal, temporary means, and he's *still* being denounced for it.[8]

More recently, we have the example of the invasion of Iraq. Hawks point to the great effects of the war: the trial of a brutal dictator, the foundation of a democratic form of government, and a more open society. Some doves point to the body count, both American troops and Iraqi civilians. More sophisticated doves argue that (a) the war wasn't just, and (b) because good flows from a thing does not make that thing right, it simply makes it less tragic.

As with war, so with hypocrisy. Spiegel explained that it may have some good effects but that doesn't make it right. It may even be the product of good, though misguided, intentions. There is a kind of "quote unquote noble hypocrisy" in which one "aims to cover up something that's a moral flaw for the sake of some other good," he said. It may be wrong, "but that isn't the sort of hypocrisy that we tend to condemn."

Now I think Spiegel is not entirely correct about that. What might have been written off as a noble sort of hypocrisy in the past—say, protecting one's church from scandal—is often held against people. Recently, condemnation of noble hypocrites has led to multimillion-dollar judgments against a certain ancient religious institution. But put that one on the backburner. What I was bursting to know is why a default judgment had been issued against hypocrisy.

Here was the gap that I saw in his thinking: Spiegel defines, in minute detail, what hypocrisy is and what it is not. It *is* deception that involves behavior. It is *not* a lie that everybody is in on, else there would be no deception. It is similar to moral weakness, except that the hypocrite is much more determined. And it often involves self-deception. It all fits together nicely. What struck me as I was rereading his first book was that this hypocrisy Spiegel was describing was not necessarily a bad thing.

On the printed page, Spiegel moved from describing hypocrisy in neutral terms to writing of it as a vice with the precision (albeit the accidental precision) of a three-card monte dealer. It took several passes until I noticed the handoff. However, there are several actions that have all the necessary ingredients of hypocrisy but to which we would be hesitant to apply the moral sanctions that are contained in the language of vice. At the very least we would apply those judgments reluctantly. Didn't this merit *some* explanation?

I asked the professor about the gap that I saw and pressed a bit. He took several stabs at an answer. Here they are in chronological order:

- Spiegel replied that he may have been "assuming that we're just talking about bad hypocrisy." By that, I assume he meant "moral hypocrisy." He reaffirmed that hypocrisy does have positive externalities and that there is a sort of noble hypocrisy that is misguided but more excusable (or less deplorable) than the selfish alternative.

- He then personalized the issue. He described parenthood as a "good laboratory for hypocrisy." There are times, he explained, "when one of my kids will challenge me on something and say, 'Well, Dad, what about this? You said this, you did that.' And I'll see that there is a kind of inconsistency there, but I'll realize that it is for the sake of a certain appearance."

- Next, he turned to politics. In statecraft, hypocrisy *could* be thought of as a necessary tool of diplomacy. In the Iran-Contra hearings, Oliver North was testifying before Congress, "coming clean on [the Reagan administration's] hypocrisy but saying, 'Look, there's a good utilitarian argument for this. You've got to watch out. The reds are going to take over. We have this perpetual danger to the south of us and even if we have to engage in underhanded kinds of strategies, it's worth it. . . . There may be a pretense of righteousness or good dealing and the fact is very different but, hey, it's justified.' If that is a plausible position, then you have a justified hypocrisy." And Spiegel allowed that what works on the institutional level may have application on the personal level as well.

- While affirming the importance of right means, he allowed that some ends "are better than others." And that some actions will be "more or less justified, though hypocritical."

- Finally, Spiegel admitted that his particularly severe introduction to hypocrisy may have gotten in the way of cold-blooded analysis. It may "explain my orientation in terms of the negativity there that could be too extreme," he said.

As I pored over the transcript of our conversation, I wondered something. In the course of the interview, Professor Spiegel may not have simply been humoring this hypocrisy obsessive. It's possible that he changed his mind. There certainly looks to be a progression in his thinking, from *It might not always be so bad* to *I could be biased.*

THE JOYS OF NIHILISM

Before readers accuse Spiegel of embracing the joys of nihilism, two things should be said in the professor's defense. One, this is my own, no doubt peculiar reading of our exchange, and I've got a few biases of my own. Two, if you admit that hypocrisy might sometimes be moral, you aren't embracing amoralism. You've simply decided to make a finer, more accurate moral distinction.

Any workable moralism has two components: the real and the ideal, or what you've got and what you want. Preachers and scolds are always tugging us from the first to the second. The early Christian missionary Paul of Tarsus spoke of the old man and the new man and urged his often exasperated followers to embrace the Brand New Me. Many moralizers pitch their reforms as a return to that old time religion, which is, among other things, a brilliant way to smuggle in a call for radical change.

"Salvation," "enlightenment," or, in modern secular psychobabble, "self-actualization." They're all meant to help move the adherents of a philosophy or religion along the trail from the valley of despair up and on to more paradisiacal vistas, from hell to heaven, vice to virtue. And hypocrisy has ended up on the "try to avoid" list for obvious reasons.

Pretentious hypocrites, in particular, may sometimes serve a useful function, but they're more to be pitied than copied. While morally serious people are making great strides, these poseurs have set up their tents somewhere along the path, where they stand and shout, denouncing the flaws of those that are leaving them in the dust.

But not all hypocrites are especially pretentious hypocrites, and not all hypocrisy deserves our considerable wrath. Some hypocrisy may be ill thought. The self-deceived hypocrite acts in his own interest and often benefits from his deceptions. But if we were to think of his defense in the familiar courtroom terms of murder, we might convict him of hypocrisy in the second or third degree, or involuntary contradiction. And some hypocrisy may be misguided but still exhibit a certain nobility. Depending on the circumstances, we might let those hypocritical offenders off with a wink and a warning.

And then there is the justified hypocrite: someone who observes the form of hypocrisy and uses it to deceive and thereby do what is right for another. We're reluctant in the first place to call this hypocrisy, because hypocrisy is a bad word, but no other term really fits. It's not moral irony. It's not moral weakness. And yet it seems like this hypocrisy is right as rain. How to make sense of it?

Start by turning the Italian civil servant on his head. The ends don't have to reach back to sanitize the unfortunate means. Hypocritical behavior can be legitimate *means* toward worthy ends. That is, I admit, a controversial statement. But many believe it to be true.

FOLLOWING YONDER STAR

Around the turn of the twentieth century, Henry Van Dyke wondered in the foreword to his remarkable short yarn, *The Story of the Other Wise Man*, "Is a lie ever justifiable?" He answered, "Perhaps not. But may it not sometimes seem inevitable?" That was an interesting thing to say, given the horrific event that it corresponded to in his story.[9]

The "other wise man" is a reference to the Magi that are a

staple of Nativity pageants at Christmastime. Van Dyke's book tells the story of yet another wise man named Artaban, who was delayed from making the pilgrimage with the rest of his caravan. He arrives in the city of Bethlehem right after a certain famous family has taken off and just before the troops of the great, ruthless King Herod arrive to dispatch a potential royal pretender by killing all the young male children.

Artaban had been taken in to a small stone hut and fed after his journey by a mother with a baby boy. When women all over town started to protest the slaughter of their sons, the wise man motioned for the mother to keep the child quiet in the corner. Then he "went quickly and stood in the doorway of the house. His broad shoulders filled the portal from side to side, and the peak of his white cap all but touched the lintel." The story continues:

> The soldiers came hurrying down the street with bloody hands and dripping swords. At the sight of the stranger in his imposing dress, they hesitated with surprise. The captain of the band approached the threshold to thrust him aside. But Artaban did not stir. His face was as calm as though he were watching the stars, and in his eyes there burned that steady radiance before which even the half tamed hunting-leopard shrinks and the fierce blood-hound pauses in his leap. He held the soldier silently for a minute, and then said, in a low voice:
>
> "I am all alone in this place, and I am waiting to give this jewel to the prudent captain who will leave me in peace."

He showed [a] jewel, glistening in the hollow of his hand like a great drop of blood.

The captain was amazed at the splendor of the gem. . . . He stretched out his hand and took the ruby.

"March on!" he cried to his men. "There is no child here. The house is still."

And they left.

Artaban may or may not be an example of justified hypocrisy. Hypocrisy is a kind of lying, but not all lies are hypocritical, just as not all birds are canaries. The claim that the wise man was all alone in the house was not, I think, intended to be taken seriously, but that didn't stop the author of the story from agonizing over the false statement.

Van Dyke decided that his character's deception was something that one might "confess" and "be pardoned for . . . more easily than for the greater sin of spiritual selfishness, or indifference, or the betrayal of innocent blood." So saving a child's life was *less bad* than not doing so.

"I CANNOT TELL A LIE"

That may sound perverse. Scratch that, to the modern ear it sounds insane. But bear in mind that current attitudes about falsehood are very different from attitudes that persisted until very recently, and still exert some force. These attitudes affect how we think of hypocrisy.

Van Dyke's story is related to an earlier one that derives from the Hebrew Bible. Before their dramatic exodus from Egypt, the decedents of Abraham faced slavery, heavy taxation, and attempted mass murder. Egyptian midwives were instructed by Pharaoh to kill every male Jewish infant, to make the people easier to dominate.[10]

The midwives refused to carry out their orders, and explained the steady rate of male childbirth by saying that it wasn't their fault. Those Jewish mothers were extraordinary. They gave birth to their boys before the midwives could cull them. These were obvious lies in the service of saving innocent lives.

Adam Nicolson recorded a few revealing reactions of various translators to the actions of the midwives in *God's Secretaries: The Making of the King James Bible*. The more explicitly Calvinist translators of the Geneva Bible had judged that the midwives' "resistance in this was lawful, but their deception is evil."[11] King James the First, titular head of the Church of England and sponsor of the book that bears his name, wouldn't even allow that their life-saving actions were lawful.

The inflexible standard on lying found its loudest champion in Saint Augustine, a fifth-century North African bishop from what is presently Algeria, who held that if a man was ailing and a truthful answer to a question would likely kill him, it was better to tell the truth and send him into the great beyond with a clear view of things. This gave new meaning to "the truth shall set you free."

Augustine's opinion was influential but not uniformly held. It was watered down by medieval scholastics, and Thomas Aquinas argued that some deceptions (including some hypocritical deceptions) were bad but not damnable. The stricter view was resuscitated by rebels, reformers, and protestors who wanted a big stick with which to bash the Catholic Church.

The church was willing to tolerate a good deal of falsehood as long as its dogmas weren't threatened, so the reformers attacked the corruption. They went after the lies and hypocrisies, and their criticisms marked Western culture indelibly, including the English colonies in North America. It changed how we think about virtue and deception.

You can see this best in Parson Weems's pious fiction about how the young Washington cut down one of his father's cherry trees and confessed to it when asked ("I cannot tell a lie.").[12] Weems's story struck a popular chord because many Americans wanted to think of the great general and statesman as someone whose character was above reproach, and whose dedication to the truth was unflinching.

That might be an unrealistic expectation for a people to have of their leaders. It seems to me, for reasons of diplomacy, that it is necessary at times for government officials to at least shade the truth, or disclaim knowledge of things that they know quite well. And yet, a message from an early Jimmy Carter campaign ad won him both the Democratic nomination and the presidency: "I will not lie to you."

Maybe it was the times. The Watergate scandal certainly helped to foment a reaction against the way that politics tends to work. However, it's useful to remember that most Americans now think of Carter as a decent and good man but a lousy president in part *because* the former governor of Georgia was unwilling to use his office to advance, through force and guile, the position of the United States on the world stage. Every single president since Carter has been much more willing to lie or behave hypocritically when the job required it, or just for the fun of it.

LAW AND DISORDER

One of the troubles with condemnations of hypocrisy is that the critics assume a just and normal order and make no exceptions for people facing unjust laws or awful circumstances. Sometimes hypocrisy is the only reasonable way of negotiating around unreasonable expectations. That is, you have to affirm something you do not believe, or only half believe, in order to do the right thing.

Walker Percy's wonderfully bitter novel *Lancelot* has as its narrator one Lancelot Andrewes Lamar, a landed gentleman from Louisiana, a Southern liberal lawyer, the last once-bright star of an old and fading family, telling his life story from the inside of an insane asylum. At one point, he relates how he faced down the Ku Klux Klan in the 1960s.[13]

The story: a cross had been burned on the lawn of a black family of the Lamar household's "ill paid retainers," the Buells, and their church had been threatened as well. The cause of the disturbance was the fact that the church (at which the elder Buell served as the part-time preacher) had allowed a civil rights group to meet on its premises.

Lamar admits that it is "true that I went to see the Grand Kleagle and the harassment stopped," but he explains that he didn't fix the problem by threatening the head Klansman. Instead, the conversation proceeded "in a manner more suited to Southern complexities and realities than the simple dreams of the sixties, when there were only good people and bad people."

Here is what happened. Lamar went to "see the Grand Kleagle all right, who was none other than J. B. Jenkins, a big dumb boy who played offensive tackle with me in both high school and college." He describes Jenkins as a "good family man [who] believed in Jesus Christ, America, the Southern way of life, hated Communists and liberals, and was not altogether wrong on any count."

Lamar asked Jenkins to lay off the Buells and their church. Jenkins protested, "Now, g—damn, Lance, you know as well as I do ain't nothing but a bunch of Jew Communists out there stirring up the niggers." Which led to a fascinating exchange:

Lamar: Will you take my word for something, J. B.?

Jenkins: You know I will.

Lamar: I swear to you there're no Jews or Communists out there [at the church] and I will swear to you that Ellis is a God-fearing Baptist like you and you have nothing to fear from him.

Jenkins: Yeah, but he is one more uppity nigger.

Lamar: Yeah, but he's *my* nigger, J. B. He's been working for us for forty years and you know that.

Jenkins: Well, that's true. Well, all right, Lance. Don't worry about nothing. Les us have a drink.

Sound far-fetched? Then answer this question: who was the politician most responsible for ending lynchings in South Carolina?

SOUTHERN DISCOMFORT

Newly elected Governor Strom Thurmond had promised during his 1946 campaign that he would "never sign a bill to mix the races," and wouldn't even consider giving blacks the right to vote. However, in his inaugural address, he did something interesting that broke with the past. He proposed more funding for black school buildings.

Thurmond's explanation for the proposal was a mix of progressive moralism and an appeal to the Southern pride of white South Carolinians: "If we provide better educational facilities for them [African-Americans], not only will much be accomplished in human values, but we shall raise our per capita income as well as the educational standing of the state."[14]

This was a politician who would run as a third party challenger to Harry Truman over the issue of segregation in 1948 and who set the record for the longest Senate filibuster over a civil rights bill in the 1950s. Still, in February of 1947, when an organized group of men beat and killed a black murder suspect in Greenville, Thurmond's legendary volcanic anger translated into quick action by law enforcement.

Journalists Jack Bass and Marilyn Thompson write that the new governor's "call for vigorous prosecution resulted in state and local police working with F.B.I. agents."[15] The massive search led to the arrests of thirty-one men. For the trial of those men, Thurmond brought in a hotshot prosecutor from nearby Spartanburg who had won convictions of 471 of 473 defendants during the previous year. Thurmond boasted to the *New York Herald Tribune*, "We in South Carolina want the world to know we will tolerate no mob violence."[16]

An all-white jury acquitted the mob, but the very public prosecution of the lynchers sent an important signal. Those would-be vigilantes who took it upon themselves to torture or kill blacks would be held up to public embarrassment and the possibility of jail. More, their actions would bring shame on all the upstanding white citizens of South Carolina. The trial served as a message that a new sheriff was in town, and he wasn't going to put up with the old mischief, and so the mischief ceased.

Thurmond was able to pull off this trick because he was seen as, and was, "one of the boys." He could work to persuade the voters of his state to behave less vilely because he espoused the same things that they believed in. Lately, Thurmond has been demonized. Trent Lott (utterly no relation) was driven from his position of majority leader of the Senate over some flattering remarks about Thurmond's presidential campaign at the elder senator's one-hundreth birthday party. Revelations that Thurmond had fathered a child by a former black maid led to more charges of racism and hypocrisy.

Thurmond was guilty of those things and more, but let it be noted that his hypocrisy allowed him to accomplish a genuine moral good. He was one of several hypocritical Southern segregationist politicians who helped to cajole white Southerners to give up Jim Crow, to convince them to accept blacks as people worthy of some considerable respect and then, finally, as equals.

The civil rights movement played the larger role in achieving full legal equality, and protesters facing down fire hoses and attack dogs make for great and good heroes. But by slowly accepting the change and selling it to white Southerners as better than the alternative, something that "we" would just have to go along with, Thurmond and company helped a worthy cause to succeed by being dignified losers.

HARD CASES, BAD HYPOCRITES

But, but, but. Let me take a moment to deal with the normal cascade of objections. The most obvious is, don't I know that hard cases make bad law? Granted, hypocrisy may be a necessary evil in really extraordinary circumstances, especially life-threatening ones, but that slope is steep and the footing tenuous. Why take the chance?

It's a fair question. The temptation is to go for the really tough cases (a) because they make better examples, and (b) because they are a way of setting people's emotions against their assumptions. But hard cases are also hard because they have the messy feeling of real life, and our ideologies don't like to put up with the clutter. It messes with our moral categories.

When we experience hypocrisy negatively, we tend to put the experiences in the mental folder labeled "hypocrisy" and add them to the growing case of why the vice is so very bad. Every time a young boy runs into a religious neighbor who promises a decent day's wage but delivers pocket change, every time a Bible-thumping televangelist is caught with a prostitute, every time a political reformer is called out for exploiting his office for private gain, the folder grows larger.

We don't normally put the good effects of hypocrisy into the same file because we don't know to look for them. "The good effects of hypocrisy" is a note, to put it mildly, that has not been sounded very often.

Think of hypocrisy like free trade. The benefits of knocking down trade barriers are spread out like butter over the toast of society. Economists assure us, and back the claim up with an impressive body of evidence, that the overall benefit is greater than the costs incurred when some people are tossed out of their jobs. It's easier to see lost jobs than economic growth and so a lot of trade skepticism persists, but there is an entire, largely tenured, group of experts to overcome any intellectual opposition, and thereby give trade a *laissez faire* chance.

Free trade has going for it a massive body of research, the entire economics profession, and many and various published attempts to defend the ends and means of the invisible hand. Hypocrisy is lucky to get the occasional obscurantist essay in its defense.

Hypocrisy is opposed by every major organized religion that I'm aware of, including the Church of Satan. Its critics include Bill O'Reilly and Dan Rather, Democrats and Republicans, most ethicists, every member of the Miss America pageant (". . . and world peace"), a majority of gas station attendants and professors of literature, and 100 percent of people with gun racks on their trucks.

However, just because most people hold the default, negative

view of hypocrisy does not stop them from behaving hypocritically. Sometimes they do it on purpose, creating a self-
consciously false appearance and using that to their own benefit.
Sometimes, Professor Spiegel argues, they try to live up to their
own standards and simply fail.

My sense is that most of us find ourselves in the vast middle
ground between those two poles, and we're not great at sorting it
out for ourselves. In his recent best-selling pamphlet, Princeton
moral philosopher Harry Frankfurt concluded that "sincerity
itself is bullshit."[17] By that he meant the judgments we make
about our own intentions and actions are often self-serving and
not anchored in anything other than what we *wish* were true. Or,
as Mafioso Tony Soprano once put it, hell is for bad people.

The upshot is that we notice hypocrisy in others, when it
offends, but not so often in ourselves. We can be unrestrained in
our judgment of hypocrisy because it does not seem that we are
passing judgment on ourselves, and also because we only see its
worst excesses and not its benefits or its virtues. This unfair sorting mechanism makes sure that we only ponder hypocrisy in the
worst possible light.

Another objection: am I arguing that everyone is a hypocrite?
Yes and no. If a hypocrite is simply someone who occasionally
behaves hypocritically, then I personally know very few nonhypocrites. If it is someone who is especially puffed up and judg-
mental, then the term applies to fewer people. But then we run
into the problem of sculpting the definition to exclude ourselves.

The popular usage of the term *hypocrite* is expansive like a
shotgun blast. It is used by Republicans to describe Democratic
officeholders who oppose publicly funded educational vouchers

but enroll their own children in private schools. It was employed to damn talk radio king Rush Limbaugh when it came out that he had a habit of popping pain pills that had been procured by questionable means, because he had once toyed with the notion that tougher sentences for drug abuse would cut down on consumption. It was charged against George W. Bush for his performance in New Orleans for reasons that were never altogether intelligible.

Hypocrite is often brought in to describe someone we don't like, doing something that we disagree with, involving some sort of perceived contradiction. It helps if there's a pattern of behavior, but that isn't a necessary part of the accusation. It's an easy charge to make and it's often annoyingly effective, because it's difficult to shrug off. It has always been a heavy judgment.

AGAINST THE GREEK CHORUS

The point of this book is to think clearly about hypocrisy, and that's not always a walk in the park. The history of the idea will run you into philosophy, psychology, even theology, all to get a hold on something that you had thought you intuitively understood. There's also etymology, the study of words. Meanings often shift as people stretch the usage of existing words into something new.

In the case of hypocrisy, the idea was breathed into an ancient Greek word that once meant something else, and it completely transformed the syllables. In Greek drama, the *hupokrites* was a speaker who spoke separately from the chorus. Used in its original context, we translate the word as "actor."

It makes a certain rough sense. Hypocrisy is acting a part. Hypocrites are "like actors, pretending to be what they are not, saying things that they do not mean, acting out parts to which they have only momentary, if any, allegiance." The words belong to Béla Szabados and Eldon Soifer, professors of philosophy at the University of Regina. The early Greek use of the term was "morally neutral," they explain, because it meant less.[18]

But nowadays the successful actor is congratulated for his convincing performance, and the hypocrite condemned. Again, that makes sense. The stage is supposed to be a world of make believe, real life much less so. But who shifted the word's meaning? What deranged theatre critic took the term and applied it as a moral judgment?

Here hypocrisy collides with historical irony. During our interview, Spiegel worried about the "widespread cynicism" that hypocrisy has "occasioned in our culture." In the past, the idea was "routinely associated with the religious," but he sensed that the resistance has grown greater, and he cited examples from headlines, film, and personal experience. Many people now use charges of hypocrisy to dismiss all traditional moralists, to wall themselves off from the reach of the religious, and to justify their own behavior. Same as it ever was, except more so.

But philosophers and historians of ideas know who it was who did the most to turn hypocrisy into Hypocrisy. They know the identity of the man who took the word and used it to lash out at his enemies. He bound it together with strident judgments so tightly that it's still difficult to untangle the moral reasoning from the disgust.

The irony is this: the man who did the most to create hypocrisy as we know it was not a freethinker or a nihilist, not an existentialist or child of the Enlightenment, not a French philosopher, and was the furthest thing from an atheist. Odds are, you've heard of him.

4

PLANK IN YOUR EYE

Let's all wash our hands as we curse hypocrites.

STEVE TAYLOR

People were used to watching disputes between teachers of the law, but this was something else. The crowd swelled in the inner court of the temple to watch a young rabbi berate his betters from early in the morning until late in the sun-baked afternoon. This man had come from nowhere, from a cow town tucked into a southern ridge of the Lebanon mountains with a population in the hundreds, if that. A rumor makes it through the rabble that he managed to get himself kicked out of even that chummy locale.

More bits of information are passed from one curious onlooker to the next, and the teacher's followers who are present do not deny these wild claims. He heals the blind and the crippled, some whisper. He multiplies loaves of bread like manna from heaven. He cast an evil spirit out of my daughter, one man insists. He offers to take doubters into the outer court to see the girl restored to her right mind.

The whispers grow louder. The rabbi quieted a storm! He called out to an old man in a tomb and the man came out! No! Yes! All true, nod the teacher's students and hangers-on. Preposterous, scoff the doubters, who throw up their hands to accentuate their words. No man could do that!

All of this is a sideshow. When they look back, observers will say that the rabbi spoke "with authority," but that fails to capture the scene except in a very blurry way. This is the second day of his unrelenting preachment against the temple management and the reigning teachers and interpreters of God's law.

Yesterday, in the outer court, this young rabbi walked up to the tables where pilgrims and peasants exchange currency stamped with Caesar's image for blank silver and bronze coins—to keep the temple treasury free of graven images—and overturned them. He drove out the cattle for sale with a whip that some say he fashioned by hand. As the moneychangers scoured the ground for the coins that had spilled everywhere, he told terrified sellers of fowl to take their caged birds and remove them from "my father's house."

Today he paces as he works the crowd. It's almost a strut, and there's that *look* in his eyes. Religious leaders try to parry his thrusts, to respond to his attacks on their credibility by questioning his. But any amateur oddsmaker can see that this is not a fair fight.

The teacher is at the peak of his substantial powers. He's cocky and whip smart and has a confidence borne of absolute conviction. If there's one thing he's ever been certain of, this is it. He seems to draw support from the temple itself, which unsettles those whose authority and livelihood are tied up in the structure.

When one old priest asks him to name the source of his own authority, the rabbi responds with a loaded question. He asks about another populist religious leader, a man recently martyred and much loved by the masses. What was the source of his authority? asks the rabbi. Answer mine and I'll answer yours.

As the afternoon wears on, it dawns on his sparring partners that the rabbi is only toying with them, and that the audience is loving it. He uses the politics and passions of the crowd to side-step questions he doesn't want to answer, to turn other questions back on his questioners, to attack their thoughts and motives. So the religious leaders stop disputing with him. They quit the scene, leaving the teacher alone with hundreds of his new best friends.

All eyes turn to the rabbi. He pauses, looks to the sky, and starts out, cautiously at first. "Those scribes and teachers of the law," he says, "they sit in the seat of Moses, so you must *listen* to them. You must pay their words special attention. But do *not* do what they do. They talk and talk and talk, but they don't *do*. They weigh your shoulders down with heavy burdens but don't lift a finger to help you carry the load."

The teacher charges that "everything they do is for show." His opponents make their prayer boxes large and their prayer tassels extra long so that "you will see these things and think well of them." They vie for the best seats at feasts and in synagogue "so that you will think them righteous." They want to be respected, to be met in the markets with the people's greetings and defer-ence. *"Rabbi have you met my youngest son?" "Rabbi, what do you think of this year's harvest?"*

He holds his hands out to quiet the laughter, and explains that this should not be the way of things. The young teacher riffs

"GIVE US A KING!"

Start with religious leaders, who are doubly vulnerable to accusations of hypocrisy. If your job is to preach, then people tend to scrutinize your life for inconsistencies. They expect you to follow your own counsel, to practice what you have just sermonized about. In fact, critics oftentimes expect you to live by stricter standards than you, or they, believe in. In the case of Bill Bennett—viewed by many as a quasi-religious leader—we saw many people who had nothing against gambling per se go after Bennett because they thought that *he* should object to gambling.

This blinkered double standard often leads to some really unfortunate results. Take pastors' families as one loaded example. My father is a Baptist minister, and I grew up in choir lofts and Christmas pageants and church potlucks. I have known scores of pastors and pastors' wives, sat through thousands of sermons, and interacted with enough fellow pastoral spawn to have formed a few of what I like to think are useful impressions about the ministry and hypocrisy.

Here's the most important one: expectations about hypocrisy often work to create actual hypocrisy. Church and community cast the pastor, his wife (or her husband), and their children in roles and all are expected to play their parts. But it rarely goes according to script, unless the play is a tragedy or a very black comedy.

In the Hebrew Bible, many sons of priests are pieces of work. Moses' brother Aaron was designated Israel's first high priest. His sons were also given formal roles, but two of them botched it. They tried to offer a sacrifice while drunk and were consumed by hellfire. Sons of the priest Eli are introduced with the charming nickname "sons of Belial." They both met a similar, though less dramatic, fate as Aaron's offspring. The sons of the priest and military leader Samuel were so awful that the Israelites demanded, "Give us a king!"[8]

The old priest tried reasoning with the crowd. He told them that a king would conscript their sons to serve in his army and their daughters to serve as bakers and ointment makers. The king would appropriate their servants and beasts of burden, and he would levy a crushing tax burden. The people weighed that dire warning against rule by the priest's sons and thus the Israeli monarchy was born.

Clearly, clerics' kids got a bad reputation early on. But Aaron, Eli, and Samuel enjoyed one advantage that most of today's Protestant ministers don't: job security. What their sons did could affect the fathers deeply. It could cause grief, or even hasten their deaths, but it could not strip them of their title or their standing vis-à-vis their religion. And the people seem to have held the fathers relatively blameless for the sins of the sons.

A preacher's kid today reads of these things with shock and awe. Nowadays, a pastor's authority derives from two sources. The first is a sense of calling. The would-be reverend believes that this is what God wants him to do, to preach and visit the sick and preside over weddings and funerals. The second part of his authority is people's recognition of his calling. And that's where things get tricky.

In some of the world's more ancient churches, you have a bureaucracy to recognize a pastor's calling, train him, and confer the appropriate authority. In the Catholic Church, a priest is a priest ultimately because Rome says so. In other churches, the authority is less centralized but still effective. Bishops create Orthodox priests. Episcopal churches are organized along similar lines. But how does one go about becoming a Baptist minister or a pastor of the local community church?

Schooling helps. Most pastors have some formal theological education. Also, churches tend to hire pastors whose beliefs are in sync with those of the selection committee. But I've caught enough stray info (i.e., gossip) over the years to believe that what really matters lies elsewhere. What really seems to do it is that the would-be pastor has the right look and feel. To put it plainly: the right image.

When they search for a new preacher, most self-governed churches are looking for a family man with (a) one supportive wife who doesn't rub people the wrong way, (b) a few well-behaved children, and (c) no divorces on his permanent record. Solid speaking skills are a must. Good looks are a major plus. Previous experience as a junior pastor doesn't hurt.

Because a preacher's image is important to his standing and future job prospects, pastors' families develop an almost Darwinian sense of public relations. They need to. Church politics can be more bruising than any political scandal. It isn't uncommon to see a large number of a church's members walk over an issue of worship, or governance, or a personality conflict, or any old thing that manages to get people's dander up. In such an unstable environment, appearances matter in a way that is hard to convey to someone who hasn't lived through it.

That terrible uncertainty is just part of the job for many pastors. Imagine trying to talk a would-be jumper down from the ledge, fifteen stories above the pavement, without a net, and you can get a pretty good picture of the problem of the modern evangelical minister's authority. It's bound up in his image, and that can easily be sent tumbling off the edge.

So, many pastors practice a moral scrupulousness in public that they do not believe in or adhere to in private. Pastors' wives tend to act as guardians and enforcers of that image. The kids are trotted out regularly and ordered to make themselves seen in the life of the church, and they had better be on their best behavior. It is preferable that the children be genuinely pious, but the appearance of piety will do just fine. The cardinal rule is: *do not embarrass us.*

OUR FATHER, WHO ART A CHILD MOLESTER

Clergy from older, more structured denominations do not face the problem of authority in quite the same way as, say, Baptists or Mennonites. But image still matters a great deal. And where image is important, accusations and loaded assumptions about hypocrisy are never far behind.

Take the sex scandals in the Catholic Church of the last several years. In 2003, I had the opportunity to interview Philip Jenkins, a professor of history and religion at Pennsylvania State University. He is the author of *Pedophiles and Priests,* a solid go-to book on clerical sexual misconduct. I badly needed some insight into the press reports and lawsuits that were threatening to tear the American arm of the Catholic Church right out of the socket, so I invited him to offer some perspective.

Studies had been done concerning the number of Catholic

priests accused of or sanctioned for sexual misconduct. I asked how big of a scandal we were looking at. How does the ratio of abusive priests stack up against, say, Protestant ministers or elementary school teachers?

"We don't know," he replied, which confounded me for a moment.

Well, then, what was our "best guess"?

Jenkins said social scientists and criminologists have a "very good idea of how many Catholic clergy are likely to be involved in sex with underage kids," in part because the Catholic Church has kept good records.

Unfortunately, Jenkins said, "nobody has ever done a worthwhile study of any other religious group or secular group involved with children, so we have to rely on impressionistic evidence." He could say with confidence only that there was no evidence that priests are more abusive than similar professionals who regularly come in contact with youths.

From detailed church records from the last fifty years, we know that four out of every one hundred priests were at some point accused of some sort of activity of a sexual nature with a minor. In a few cases, this simply involved an exchange of words or the use of images that were deemed pornographic. Over half of cases involved the sometimes murky category of inappropriate touching. Slightly less than a quarter of the accusers alleged penetration or attempted penetration.

According to a report by the John Jay College of Criminal Justice, "only a small percentage of priests receiv[ed] allegations of abusing young children." Six percent of the allegations concerned children six years old and younger. Slightly over half of all accused priests were accused of any kind of abuse one time only. A very small minority of allegedly abusive priests (between 3 and 4 percent) racked up more than a quarter of the total caseload.[9]

It was the serial offenders who really got the ball rolling. Massachusetts-based priest John Geoghan was not a one-time groper but a genuine, serial pedophile. As the *Boston Globe* explained in its earth-shattering investigative report, "Almost always, his victims were grammar school boys. One was just four years old." And there were more than 130 people alleging abuse: rape, forced masturbation, you name it.[10]

The Geoghan story was explosive in part because the abuse had not escaped the notice of church higher-ups. It had gone on with their knowledge and, critics argued, with their support. The Boston archdiocese had transferred Geoghan from one parish to the next and worked to keep his misbehavior quiet. He was allowed to use his position to abuse little boys for thirty-four years, under three different archbishops, against the vigorous objections of victims and even high-ranking church officials.

Geoghan was the most notorious case, but this method for dealing with priestly sexual abuse allegations used to be widespread. In order to avoid public scandal, church officials had worked hard to keep accusations from being aired. They often appealed to the religion of the parents, with the troubling implication that a good Catholic would not bring embarrassment upon the church, for *any* reason. Failing that, one precondition of a monetary settlement was an ironclad confidentiality agreement.

Offending priests were often reassigned elsewhere, shuffled from parish to parish. Their new superiors were rarely informed of their history, which made future abuse much more likely. Occasionally, care was taken to make sure that problem priests weren't placed in the orbit of the young, but the results were mixed. As the *Globe* reported, Geoghan was eventually assigned to assist at a home for retired priests, "but even that decision . . . did not prevent him from seeking out and molesting children."

This explosive local story received national attention and thus began what Jenkins describes as a "moral panic," a perfect storm of outrage and self-interest. The reports emboldened more people, in Boston and elsewhere, to come forward with allegations of abuse. Reporters in other locales went looking for errant priests and found more than a few. Trial lawyers launched multi-million-dollar lawsuits and tried to uncover more clients by subpoenaing church records.

Several state legislatures responded to the call to "do something" by lengthening the statute of limitations to report sexual abuse. These looser statutes gave the trial lawyers and new victims' rights groups more leverage against dioceses all over the country. They would use that leverage to great effect.

THE NEXT CHAPTER 11

"[A]bout 700 priests and deacons have been removed from ministry in Catholic dioceses since January, 2002." That's according to the U.S. Conference of Catholic Bishops, and the statistic is slightly dated.[11] By the time you read this, the figure will be closer to 1,000. The current president of the Conference, Bishop William Skylstad of Spokane, Washington, was elected by his fellow American princes of the church in the wake of his diocese declaring bankruptcy to protect church assets from abuse victims.[12]

The Spokane diocese was one of a handful to file for bankruptcy, but dozens thought about it. New Boston Archbishop Sean O'Malley used the threat of Chapter 11 to finally force the holdouts to settle, and bishops in other locales also employed similar legal tactics.

After Spokane declared bankruptcy, spokesmen for the Seattle archdiocese noted "with deep regret" that such a thing had to occur on the other side of the mountains, and then put the following message to trial lawyers. So far Seattle had settled cases for "fair and reasonable amounts." It did not "anticipate the need to consider bankruptcy protection" as long as the insurance companies cooperate and future settlements remain "fair and reasonable." Translation: don't push your luck, guys.[13]

As a bluff, bankruptcy helped to keep the settlements in the hundreds of thousands of dollars per alleged victim rather than in the millions. But going through with bankruptcy hasn't turned out so well for Spokane. A federal bankruptcy judge refused to consider parish and school assets as separate from diocesan assets. Attorneys for the victims pointed out that the over $80 million in judgments could be paid if, say, the diocese would sell off schools and parishes.

Two anonymous plaintiffs had brought suit separately against the archdiocese of Portland, Oregon. They demanded a total of $153 million and refused to settle. The cases were both to come to trial in July 2004. The archdiocese responded on the day of the first trial by filing for bankruptcy protection.

Portland Archbishop John Vlazny explained in a letter to local

Catholics that while he was "committed to just compensation," the amounts being demanded were a king's ransom from a relative pauper's purse. "I cannot in justice and prudence pay the demands of these two plaintiffs," he wrote.[14]

As the Portland case slowly made its way through bankruptcy courts, the Spokane ruling opened up the diocese to the prospect of having to sell off schools and parishes. In response, lawyers for the diocese did something that was, on the face of it, insane. They named each and every one of the 390,000 or so Catholics in Western Oregon as class-action codefendants.[15]

There was a method to this malarkey. The stated purpose was not to open rank-and-file Catholics to massive liabilities but to teach the courts something about church structure and church governance. The Portland archdiocese was trying to send a message to the judges about the limits of liability. It was a *reductio ad lawsuitum*.

Attorneys for the alleged abuse victims were not amused and not in a mood to show any mercy. According to the Eugene daily, the *Register-Guard*, up to a point individual Catholics could opt out of the class action defense. But most did not do so because the plaintiffs' lawyers "have said they probably will name any parishioner who opts out as an individual defendant."[16]

Legal wrangling in Portland and elsewhere will continue for some time, and lawyers' fees and settlements will continue to climb. It's next to impossible to get a handle on what the final price tag will look like. John Jay College estimated that "the total cost paid by the church exceeds $500 million." That was as of February 2004, and the researchers admitted it was probably a significant undercount of the funds *already paid*.

Claims against just the Oregon archdiocese come to over $400 million.

The money has to come from somewhere, and the "somewhere" is often parishes, Catholic schools, and goods and services meant for the poor. One Eugene churchgoer, faced with the real possibility of losing most of the parishes and parochial schools in the Western half of Oregon, tried to look on the bright side of life.

"If that happens, it happens—it's not going to change my faith in God," said retired businessman Dennis Murphy. "Give to Caesar what is Caesar's and give to God what is God's—and if the church belongs to Caesar, give it to him."[17]

"THEY'RE WORSE THAN POLITICIANS"

I rehash the details of the Catholic sex scandals and the rash of lawsuits that followed for a reason. The situation lies at the bloody crossroads of hypocrisy, outrage about hypocrisy, and painful experience.

Catholic dioceses are opting for the previously unprecedented choice of bankruptcy because they have a poor track record in the courtroom. If sex abuse cases make it to trial, the dioceses tend to lose and lose big. In one case, a jury awarded eleven plaintiffs just shy of $120 million. In another, two plaintiffs—brothers, it turns out—secured a $30 million judgment.[18]

Huge judgments are often reduced by courts or negotiated down by plaintiffs if the other party threatens to seek bankruptcy protection, but the more interesting question is why do juries render such whopping verdicts against the Catholic Church? The answer appears to be moral revulsion. And the target of this revulsion is largely the church's hypocrisy.

Time and again, jurors who are willing to talk after trials say they're disgusted that the abuse was committed by *priests* and covered up by so-called men of God. One juror said of most of the clerics who testified before him, "They're worse than politicians."[19] And the trial lawyers, of course, egg them on. With 40 percent of a multimillion-dollar judgment on the line, you would too. The plaintiffs' lawyers tell jurors to "send a message" to the Vatican. Tell them we'll no longer put up with this sort of two-faced, reprehensible behavior.

In newspaper columns, on television and talk radio, and all over the Internet, people who disagree with Catholic norms began to use the sex scandals to shout the church down. Didn't Jesus say it would be better to be drowned in the ocean with a millstone tied around your neck before you bring harm to a little child? Where, the critics wanted to know, does Rome get off lecturing us about abortion and homosexuality and war when its vision is obscured by the rather large issue of child molestation?

Most people will think that a good question, so allow me to press it further to illustrate why it isn't. Where do public schools get off teaching "our" children how to behave when a certain number of teachers every year will be caught in bed with students and some of it will be covered up?

Sex between teachers and students is not a small problem. A Department of Education survey of sexual misconduct studies found (a) that we don't have good national numbers on teacher-student sexual misbehavior, but (b) what evidence we do have is troubling. According to one lowball extrapolation, "more than 4.5 million students [of American public schools] are subject to sexual misconduct by an employee of a school sometime between kindergarten and twelfth grade."[20]

And sexual abuse is rarely a one-off affair. According to G. Robb Cooper, an Illinois-based education attorney, abusive teachers are rarely caught right away. "Every instance that I have dealt with, there has been a repeat offence," he told me.[21]

So I'll return to my question. Don't the Mary K. Letourneaus of this world put the lie to the entire system of public schooling? Don't the abuses that take place within elementary, middle, and high schools prove the whole enterprise a mistake?

You might be tempted to shrug those questions off with an *Of course not. Don't be ridiculous.* OK, but why not? And why should comparable abuses in the Catholic Church be treated as an earth-shattering crisis, worthy of much finger-wagging, soul-searching, and crushing punitive damages, especially since the worst of it was demonstrably over?

MILLSTONES AND MILESTONES

The really startling thing, as I combed through the data on clerical sexual abuse of minors, was the realization that any larger "crisis" was long past us. According to John Jay College, the number of reported abuse cases peaked in 1970. The authors of the report argued that some of the abuse in the '70s was really extensive, so they suggested grading on the curve by resetting the peak at 1980.

In English, the number of abuse cases began to decline after

1970, and the severity of the abuse started plummeting the same year that Ronald Reagan was elected president. Even with the recent stampede of new reports of abuse, the John Jay criminologists noted that "the allegations of abuse in recent years are a *smaller share* of all allegations."

That it's-getting-better-all-the-time figure works well with the distribution of accused priests. Those ordained between 1950 and 1979 managed to draw almost 70 percent of the total number of allegations. Those priests ordained after 1979 attracted just a hair over 10 percent of all allegations.[22]

If we were to paint by the numbers, the picture of the last twenty-five years would portray a gradual weeding out of abusive priests from parishes and payrolls of American Catholic dioceses. Pockets of reported abuse persisted, but even John Geoghan was transferred out of a role that put him in contact with children in 1993 and then defrocked by Pope John Paul II in 1998.

The reasons for the decline in abusive priests are not always easy to grasp. Over the last twenty-five years, we've undeniably had a better "crop" of priests than those who preceded them, but stating that fact doesn't begin to answer the question: why? Litigation and criminal prosecutions no doubt made some difference in making people aware of abuse, but legal threats often had the opposite effect of what you might expect.

For example, a Philadelphia grand jury issued a report last year claiming that retired Archbishop Anthony Bevilacqua was, basically, evil. But jurors lamented that Bevilacqua was also an evil *genius*. They argued the archbishop had used his knowledge of the law to build a well-oiled machine to shelter abusive priests, generate reams of plausible deniability, and run out the clock on statutes of limitations. Under current law, the grand jury couldn't bring an indictment.[23]

So *what was it* that led to the falloff in abuse-of-minors claims? I took this question to a Protestant minister who asked to remain anonymous. He told me that, in the late '70s, the youth ministry team at his church ran into a problem. The ministry had relied on several volunteers to lead Bible studies, organize events for junior high and high school youths, and provide supervision for trips and summer camps.

At one particular summer camp, the pastor told me, something bad happened. One volunteer from his church who was serving as a camp counselor was caught in bed with a few junior-highers. Some touching was involved and maybe worse.

"It was a real mess," he said.

"What did they do?" I asked.

"They pulled him out of camp, read him the riot act, and removed him from any position where he would be overseeing kids," he answered. "And then we all watched him like a hawk."

But the hawk eventually circled away and the former volunteer found a way to get at more youths in the same church that had promised to keep a close eye on him. A few years ago, the pastor received word that the law had finally caught up with the man. He was convicted in the '90s on several counts of child molestation.

"How did that happen?" I asked, a little stunned.

The reverend explained that while the original group of volunteers and a few others who knew, including him, were still at the church, "we could make sure that he wasn't allowed anywhere near kids. But then, one by one, we all moved away. And he went right back to it."

Nowadays, the pastor said, he'd call the cops in a New York minute. He would do so because he'd been burned once but also because he's learned something about child abusers in the last few decades.

"They're a menace. They can't control themselves," he said. "I'm not saying you should kill child abusers, but you should definitely lock them away on an island, away from the rest of us, away from children, for the rest of their lives."

The pastor's experience mirrors the experience of the country as a whole. I know it's hard to imagine in an era when you have to be fingerprinted, pee in a cup, and submit to checks by the FBI, the FAA, and the NAACP to volunteer to hand out Fudgsicles in your daughter's kindergarten class, but the sexual abuse of minors used to be dealt with privately in many cases. Friends or relatives of the abused would move to box the abuser in, to add more supervision and limit his access to kids, or just to get him to pack up and move on.

The private option was based on two notions. The admirable reason was that parents and others wanted to keep minors from having to rehash the details of their abuse in front of dozens of people. It's bad enough to be raped or molested. To have to relive the details in a courtroom and to withstand the cross-examination of lawyers for the defense can be really horrifying. The other notion was that abusers can change.

Over the last few decades, the country has moved away from the "abusers can change" model. The rates of recidivism for sex offenders are just too high to ignore, and the stories of abuse too gruesome. Public opinion has swung in favor of more punitive measures, and lawmakers have come up with a patchwork of laws and measures aimed at addressing the concern: sex offender registries, post-prison detention, rape shield laws.

The Catholic Church had moved in the same direction as the rest of the country and was continuing apace. Dioceses slowly developed policies and reflexes to treat sexual abuse by priests not as a pastoral issue but as a crime. The seminaries did a better job of screening candidates, and errant priests were given less slack. Many of the older, harder-to-get-at priests were nonetheless being weeded out. At most, the sex scandals that began in 2002 only sped up a process that was well underway.

THE SOFT TYRANNY OF HIGH EXPECTATIONS

Many Catholics had an intuitive sense that things were improving, and they resented the fact that abuse from the '70s and '80s and earlier was being dredged up now and used to bloody the church's image. Charges of bias became a regular staple of the response to what nearly everybody was calling a crisis. Retired Archbishop Bevilacqua, for instance, charged the grand jury with hostility to Catholicism even though several grand jurors were Catholics and they went out of their way *not* to frame their findings as an indictment of the faith.

A few of those who covered the sex scandals may have had it in for the hierarchy of the Catholic Church, but that was, and remains, beside the point. Something much larger was at work: the soft tyranny of high expectations. The reason that so much attention was focused on the scandals of the church, not just in

Boston but all over the country, was the contradiction between ideal and real, word and deed, faith and practice.

Reporters and readers were sucked in to an old familiar narrative. People managed to get much more worked up than usual about allegations of abuse that took place fifteen or thirty years ago because of who had done the abusing, and who had allowed it to happen. As with the Bennett case, hypocrisy was a good way to organize and sell the story, and to lash thousands of reports together as part of One Big Story.

In fact, the outrage could be interpreted as a painfully backhanded compliment. The cases of abuse that are uncovered in public schools are not roped together as part of a larger crisis because people have come to expect and demand less from our schools. The Catholic Church, by contrast, has never really tried to disguise its moralism or mask its intention to shape minds and have a say in how we should live.

By stumping for absolute, unchanging virtues, the church opened itself up to charges of and expectations about hypocrisy. As tales of woe rolled off the presses, flickered across our television screens, or orated through our courtrooms, we certainly saw plenty of hypocrisy. Most Americans were interested and disgusted, but for some that disgust was tempered by experience and a sense of dread.

The evangelical newsmagazine *World* responded to the Catholic sex scandals by running a "don't be smug"-type cover story. The magazine's largely conservative Protestant audience learned that a "disturbing pattern of sexual exploitation is afoot in some churches, including churches that generally teach biblical truth."[24] The "pattern" claim was a bit of overstatement, but *World* did manage to lash enough tales of pastoral abuse together to make the point that sex abuse wasn't merely a Catholic problem.

If religions were buildings, the Catholic Church would be the tallest structure in the United States. It's the single largest denomination and the oldest one. It has lines of authority that crisscross much of the globe. Its stature makes it a lightning rod for accusations of hypocrisy, but this same dynamic often plays out in miniature in the lives of countless churchgoers of all denominations.

The problem of hypocrisy falls hardest on clerics and their families. It also weighs down those who attend church with some regularity or do things that give the appearance of piety: pray at meals, decorate their homes or offices with religious artifacts, read scripture. Many who want to observe their religion quietly find that they might as well be shouting from a soapbox for all the scrutiny they receive.

Worse, believers find that a certain preacher from Nazareth is on the side of the antihypocritical scoffers. But only very superficially.

WHOM WOULD JESUS DENOUNCE?

Kathy Shaidle is a poet and author, and a friend. She's a lightning-quick wit and a terror if you ever have the misfortune of squaring off against her on television, a sort of blonde Catholic Ayn Rand with an Eastern Canadian accent. So when her attention turned to hypocrisy, my ears perked up.

It came in the middle of one of her many controversies. Shaidle was giving an essayist what-for for being "overly concerned with hypocrisy," a vice that, she smirked, had "replaced murder" sometime around the Edwardian era as "*the* unforgivable sin in the minds of enlightened intellectual sophisticates."[25]

"Yes," she admitted, "Jesus cursed the Pharisees as hypocrites in one of his most scathing addresses—but he was mad about *the bad stuff the Pharisees were doing,* not the fact that they were being hypocrites about it all."

Shaidle was about half right, but it's the most important half. Jesus violently disagreed with many teachers of the law about their reading of said law. But the bone that he couldn't swallow was that they were far too self-serving in their reading, not necessarily that they were too demanding.

Jesus chastised the teachers for many actions, but he also embarrassed them for the things that they *didn't do.* The young rabbi called them out for placing the weight of God's law on people's shoulders but refusing to put their backs to it.

In this at least, the rabbi does not find common cause with our many modern antihypocrites. Those critics who hold religious leaders and ordinary churchgoers to some standard—and often an absurd standard at that—while they shrug off any moral burden for themselves are simply the flip side of the same hypocritical coin.

Let me put it another way to tease out the point. If the teachers of the law had ceased to teach and the priests had locked up the temple, would the preacher from Nazareth have said, *Well, at least they aren't being hypocrites?* Not unless he suddenly decided to depart from the tone and tenor of *everything* he'd ever said in public. The Jesus of the Gospels would have raged against them twice as hard for abandoning even the trappings of religion.

Much of what was once labeled "higher criticism" of the Gospel stories painted Jesus as an almost modern liberal critic of a rigid social and religious order. More recent scholarship has pointed out that Jesus viewed himself as an authentic teacher of the law who always claimed to be speaking from within the great tradition of his people. The second approach makes more sense to me for historical as well as aesthetic reasons. I've tried to reproduce the approach here because it seems to best capture the strangeness of the rabbi from Nazareth.

It's hard for people in this day and age to understand how Jesus could tell the crowd (a) that the teachers of the law were a bunch of brazen hypocrites, but that (b) the people still had to listen to them and, to a large extent, respect their authority as preachers and interpreters of the faith. But, according to the book of Matthew, that's exactly what he said.

Following in Jesus's lead, the church's stock response to hypocrisy is different from the modern reaction in a few important ways. One, it holds that the hypocrite's sin lies not in the preaching but in the doing or not doing. The deed is the thing. Two, it treats hypocrisy as one of many sins rather than as the one ethical infraction that's worthy of our anger. Three, it allows for and, in fact, encourages forgiveness.

According to the world's most famous rabbi, if the hypocrite stops behaving badly and lives up to his own high standards, that's as it should be. God's in heaven, all's right with the world, roll the credits.

5

WALK THE TALKIES

Make it ten. I'm only a poor corrupt official.

CAPTAIN RENAULT

Ed Asner is a veteran television actor and the former two-term president of the Screen Actors Guild.[1] His most famous character was Lou Grant, the acerbic newspaper boss on the *Mary Tyler Moore Show*. Apart from his paid work, Asner has often taken on the role of celebrity spokesman for various causes. He's spoken out against racism in American society[2] and in favor of a new trial for convicted cop-killer Mumia Abu-Jamal,[3] against the United States' backing of anti-Communist insurgents in Central America[4] and in favor of more disclosure by the U.S. government about "what really happened" on September 11.[5]

Asner was one of several prominent business and civic leaders that the new economy-oriented magazine *Fast Company* queried for their thoughts on "giving back" to the community. He replied that the "greatest service" one can render is to "expose hypocrisy, question authority, and blow the whistle." These provocations, he said, "are not popular activities." In fact, there are real "punishments" in store for those who speak up. As far as cutting checks goes, Asner argued that it requires "no courage at all to give your name or your money to the symphony orchestra."[6]

Many actors share Asner's view. There's nothing wrong with a star donating his own money, understand. But they see it as almost beside the point because they can make a greater impact by loaning their celebrity to pet causes. That self-important assumption has often left a bad taste in people's mouths, but it's not necessarily wrong. The reason that companies constantly offer barrels full of money to movie stars to advertise products is that celebrity endorsements cause fans and admirers to sit up and take notice. People who read *People* are highly suggestible.

Barbra Streisand probably needs no introduction. Her singing, songwriting, and acting precede her, as do her liberal politics. Matt Stone and Trey Parker, creators of the laughalicious anticelebrity cartoon *South Park*, have called her everything they hate about Hollywood wrapped in one petite package.[7] She has become a familiar villain to conservatives for her statements casting the red team in the worst possible light and extolling the virtues of liberal governance.

Babs has raised a lot of money for liberal causes over the years. She also has a proven record of generating headlines and provoking loud, angry reactions from Republicans to counter her barbs. Both activities are valuable to her party, but by my own rough calculus, her outspokenness is probably the greater contribution.

Streisand wrote on her own Web site about the Rathergate scandal,[8] in which CBS underlings had put together a report on the basis of documents that were fraudulent to charge that President Bush had ducked out of his mandatory National Guard service. A number of anachronisms should have raised flags that the document was forged, especially the superscripted *th*'s. (On today's computers, it isn't difficult to get, say, 11th to come out as 11th, but most typewriters from the 1970s didn't have that capability.) When the obvious forgery came to light, long-time anchorman Dan Rather was forced into early retirement.

If that punitive response was warranted, sputtered Streisand, then so was impeachment, because the Bush administration's alleged "lies were far more serious and detrimental to the American public in that it falsely represented the reasons to wage war [in Iraq] and send young soldiers into battle. . . . The hypocrisy would be laughable, if it wasn't so tragic."[9]

Set aside the question of whether you agree with the song-bird from Brooklyn. Ask instead what would be more valuable to Democratic candidates: a month of Streisand futzing around on her own Web site or a $100,000 donation? Bear in mind that what she writes will be echoed by supporters and readers who share her point of view, denounced by Republicans, and possibly quoted in news accounts and chopped up as sound bites on cable and network news. Not bad publicity if you can get it.

Take the example of John Cusack, leading man of hit movies since the 1980s with a giant bone to pick with George W. Bush. Anybody could badmouth the president, but when Cusack spoke up in the summer of 2001, it made headlines. In a cover story for *Details* magazine, Cusack predicted that Bush was "gonna do a lot of damage" and bashed the "crypto-fascists" now in power.

Bush, Cusack explained, is "this great symbol of inversion to me—the inverse of the truth. It's like the ethics of the new millennium. All you have to do is say something and it's true. 'I'm Muslim.' But you don't actually ever go to a mosque. You don't have to give up pork. You don't have to do anything. You just say it. That's the level of the hypocrisy and stupidity that's going on right now."[10]

His protests worked their way through the media food chain. The *New York Daily News* reported the story under the headline "Apparently, Being John Cusack Means Being Really Mad at Bush."[11] When a promotional interview for the *Washington Post* the next month started to go nowhere, the reporter suggested that he could spice things up by "slamming a Republican" and Cusack made with the outrage.[12]

THE HOLLYWOOD PARADOX

These examples point to the Hollywood Paradox. Many observers see Hollywood as a den of iniquity: Sodom, Gomorrah, and Las Vegas rolled into one and bet on black-seventeen. The tabloids provide a regular downpour of tawdry details to add to this impression, and there is some evidence that a great number of actors and related professionals see their own industry as corrupt on a fairly massive scale.

At the 2006 Academy Awards, host John Stewart told his star-studded audience, "A lot of people say that this town is too liberal, out of touch with mainstream America, an atheistic pleasure dome, a modern-day, beachfront Sodom and Gomorrah, a moral black hole where innocence is obliterated in an endless orgy of sexual gratification and greed." His punch line elicited nervous laughter: "I don't really have a joke here. I just thought you should know a lot of people are saying that."[13]

At the same time, many Hollywood alums are loudly moralistic. Actors regularly and unironically attempt to "make a difference" or "change the world," in ways great and small. They lend their proven ability to generate headlines to causes that run the gamut from literacy programs to AIDS prevention to political campaigns to environmental concerns, with sometimes ridiculous results.

Hollywood's cause mentality is often mocked, even by people in the industry. In a 1997 interview, comedian and television actor Drew Carey told the libertarian monthly *Reason* magazine that his involvement with the homeless benefit Comic Relief was really for his own betterment.

"[I]t's a badge of honor as a comedian to do that show," Carey explained. "Comic Relief does a lot of good but homeless people really bug the hell out of me. They're smelly, they're always asking me for money. I like to help out, but I also do this in my act where I say, 'I don't know how much money we raised to help the homeless tonight, but the food backstage was great.'"

The food, he said, was "all gourmet-catered, all the drinks were free, not a homeless guy in sight. Everyone in Hollywood comes to these things and then says, 'Look how we cured homelessness.' They feel guilty if they party and there's not a good reason for it. If you had the same show with all the best comedians and no charity involved, they'd be like, 'Uh-oh, can't do that.' They want to make themselves look good—a lot of it is about feeding egos."

Carey confessed that he didn't see himself as "some sort of political type like Alec Baldwin or Barbra Streisand." In fact, he would be "embarrassed if that was the way I came across." Then he affected concern: "I should watch what I say about Streisand: she could call a congressman, not have my garbage picked up anymore, change my zoning laws, totally screw me over."

The Cleveland comic acknowledged the promise and the problem of star power. On the one hand, he admitted, it can do some good, focus people's attention, raise money, even change a few lives. But then there are the problems of motive and misrepresentation. When Carey voiced skepticism about doing an appearance on behalf of the American Cancer Society, the interviewer asked, "So you're in favor of cancer?"

Carey countered that he was in favor of "*not* inflating your ego, of only doing good deeds to pump yourself up. Which is about as anti-Hollywood, as anti-celebrity as you can get." But he also said that he wished that there were more organizations like Comic Relief, as a private, voluntary way to help hard-up people out.[14]

Of course, these wished-for organizations would have to trade on special treatment and ego inflation to get spokesmen who could raise funds.

TWO STEPS FORWARD, BUT . . .

They may bristle at this characterization, but actors who lend their celebrity to causes are in the moral improvement business. They aim to better the conditions and behavior of their fellow men. Moral reformers almost uniformly condemn hypocrisy, but their success encourages more hypocrisy by inviting imitators.

Most people take it to be a good thing that entertainment professionals work to raise money to fund soup kitchens and homeless shelters and the like. If a comedian appears regularly in fundraisers, our estimation of that comic is likely to rise. *He's such a nice guy. He's civic-minded. He gives back to the community.*

That may be an accurate impression or it may be very far off the mark. As Carey said, the comedian is also acting in his self-interest. He receives more than warm fuzzies from his performance. He gets exposure, television time, or other free advertisements. He gets a paid trip and hotel accommodations and food. He may earn a favor that he can call in later. People think better of him just for doing his routine.

The potential for hypocrisy in this sort of situation is great. For instance, in addition to travel and lodging, celebrities are often paid to "volunteer" their time and name to charities.

Given the number of organizations looking to trade on the names of entertainers, you can understand why an actor would charge for face time, if only to cut down on the number of appearances. But to accept compensation from charities for flacking, as many do, blurs the line between civic-minded citizens and paid spokesmen.

Perhaps the most compelling objection to hypocrisy is the free rider problem. Someone superficially imitates virtue as a way to convince others to think better of him and then uses those ill-formed thoughts to further his own interests. He gets the benefits of virtue (a good reputation) without having to take on any of the costs (upright behavior even when other people aren't looking). Remember the last chapter: A certain rabbi accused many teachers of the law of loading people down with obligations but then refusing to help carry the load.

As with Pharisees, so with celebrities. It isn't at all uncommon for stars to demand large speaking fees from the same organizations that are "honoring" them for "giving back" to the community. To get paid to have people praise your selflessness has got to rank as one of the great hustles of all time.[15]

But sometimes a little hypocrisy is part of getting the job done. Charities understand that they will only receive a percentage of the funds raised and yet they still agree to hold the speeches and galas. They do so for the same reason that companies are willing to shell out money to employ celebrity spokesmen: they can bring in the crowds and rake in the dollars.

If speaking fees and massive ego-stroking are necessary to make this happen, so be it. And if people are under the mistaken impression that the speakers are volunteering their time, well, that helps to hold down the speaking fees.

In his best-selling book *Do As I Say (Not As I Do): Profiles in Liberal Hypocrisy*, the conservative Hoover Institution's Peter Schweizer takes aim at a number of liberal icons, including Barbra Streisand and guerilla documentarian and author Michael Moore.[16] Schweizer gets in a lot of decent jabs, but his shots don't always connect, especially when he swings at charitable donations.

In the case of Moore, the back cover of the book features what promises to be a great *gotcha!* moment. Under a quote by Moore explaining that "I don't own a single share of stock," we see a disclosure form that lists stocks bought and sold. Shares of

Boeing, Xerox, and Honeywell are among the liquidated stocks, and shares of controversial defense contractor Halliburton are highlighted in yellow. The signature on the document belongs to one Michael Moore.

The *got* never quite manages to *cha!* because Moore doesn't own these stocks. They are the property of a private charitable foundation that he set up to fund causes that he thinks important. Underneath the headline was a story about how philanthropy can be berry berry good for business. Moore publicly says that the foundation funds "first-time filmmakers, battered women's shelters, and soup kitchens, among other things."[17] It does issue some modest grants for those things, and will likely issue more and larger grants in response to the bad press that Schweizer's book has occasioned.

You see, Moore's foundation grants have tended overwhelmingly to further his own interests. He's given cash to film societies that helped to promote his documentaries. Money was lavished on friends and colleagues who are already well-established in the business, and in a position to repay the favor. And Schweizer speculates that a gift of $25,000 to the American Library Association was a big *thank you* for the role that organization played in getting publisher HarperCollins to rethink its decision to cancel one of Moore's books after September 11.

The author of *Stupid White Men* knows who his friends are, and that consideration helps to determine who gets foundation money. He invests some foundation funds in the stock market as a way of earning returns on the money rather than letting it idle. That those things are regarded as scandalous is kind of puzzling.

"CANADIAN BEER SUCKS"

Moore's foundation is controversial for two reasons. It is controversial, first, because many people expect charity to be selfless. The giver is doing a good thing, quite apart from any airy-fairy considerations of self-interest. Ideally, one should give because it is the right thing to do.

The reality has always been more mixed, especially when the givers have a lot of money. Andrew Carnegie and other titans of industry have done some really phenomenal things over the years, including building our great public libraries. No doubt, good feelings for their fellow men played a role in that. But so did the bottom line. By giving so much back over the years, the well-off have managed to convince the more numerous less well-off not to confiscate too much of their wealth.

Second, Schweizer has taken to arguing in interviews that the foundation's holdings are evidence of Moore's hypocrisy. To my mind, he has a point on this one. Michael Moore may not "own" stock, but he is a former editor of the anticorporate monthly magazine *Mother Jones,* and his career is built on the use of the documentary to expose the lies and evasions of big business and government officials.

In his one work of admitted fiction, the movie *Canadian Bacon*, director Moore paints a paranoid fantasy of industrialist R. J. Hacker (played by G. D. Spradlin) manipulating a hapless liberal president (Alan Alda) to the brink of war with Canada, and also to the brink of nuclear annihilation. It's a funny, underappreciated movie with a lot of great lines ("What? All I said was 'Canadian beer sucks.'" "We got ways of making you pronounce the letter 'O.'"). But it also expresses Moore's basic view of society.

Moore believes that big business is evil and predatory and that government is a tool of big business. Connected to his conspiratorial view of how the world works is his conviction that the stock market is a scam to fleece suckers. It's simply a way for the rich to convince the poor to give them money in exchange for empty promises of higher returns.

But Moore went and invested foundation funds in the stock market. Why? If you thought it was a scam, you wouldn't invest in it, right? The foundation investments call Moore's anti-big business posture into question, don't they? What kind of self-respecting anti-corporate crusader damns business but then sinks hundreds of thousands of dollars into the stock market?

A hypocritical one, Schweizer argues, and it seems right. There is a massive disconnect between Moore's public preachments and his private behavior.

Then again, I could be wrong, just as I argue many people were wrong to label Bill Bennett a hypocrite. Schweizer never offers good evidence that Moore has his own personal holdings, and it's possible that Moore views the foundation investments as a sort of poetic justice. That is, he wants to use monies reaped from the stock market to finance antimarket causes, such as anti-big business documentaries by other filmmakers. It's a stretch, but it could be consistent with his impish sense of vengeance.

Schweizer divides hypocrisy into two types: liberal (i.e., "cause") hypocrisy that is common to Hollywood, academia, and the Democratic Party; and plain-vanilla hypocrisy ("conservative hypocrisy") for the rest of us. He argues that liberal hypocrisy is the worse of the two because conservatives usually "confine their moral beliefs to the realm of personal conduct and responsibility" while liberals seek to turn their moralism into legislation.

Charging liberals with "legislating morality" is a nice bit of rhetorical jujutsu. Schweizer takes an accusation that has been used against conservatives for years and attempts to turn it back on the critics. He's right to insist that liberals can be every bit as controlling as conservatives, but then he tries to ignore attempts by conservatives to do things like ban abortion, force new crackdowns on illegal drugs, and discourage illegitimacy.

Looking at what was labeled the "values vote" from the 2004 elections, my friend Jesse Walker, anarchist author of *Rebels on the Air*, wrote that fears about evangelical voters were far too limited and self-serving. In fact, there was a whole lot more to be afraid of in the American political ferment and not just from evangelicals.

Walker explained that there is "no party of tolerance in Washington—just a party that wages its crusades in the name of Christ and a party that wages its crusades in the name of Four Out Of Five Experts Agree."[18]

Schweizer argues that the two varieties of hypocrisy are treated differently. "Conservatives who abandon their principles and engage in hypocrisy usually end up harming themselves and their families," he writes. "[L]iberals who do the same usually benefit."[19]

They're allowed to eat their cake and have it too, you see, and we can't have that. Fairness demands that we hold liberals to the same . . . to the same . . . to . . . zzzzzzzzzzzzzzzz zzzzzzzzzzzzzzzzzzzzzzzzzzzzzzzzzzzzzzzzzzzzzzzzzzzzz

Sorry.

Nodded off there for a minute.

Do As I Say (Not As I Do) is worth reading, but if there is a more tiresome trope than partisan accusations of unfairness, I've missed it.

The fact is that hypocrisy accusations are a regular part of the rhetoric of the Hollywood left and also of the anti-Hollywood right. Socially involved celebrities charge their opposite numbers with hypocrisy, and conservatives aren't shy about returning fire. Right-wing talk radio hosts from Rush Limbaugh to Sean Hannity to Michael Savage constantly call liberals hypocrites as a way of tearing them down.

It's on old, familiar routine. Both sides attempt to downplay their own hypocrisy and play up the hypocrisy of opponents for political gain or to feel better about themselves or just for spite.

And though they may disagree about everything else, all parties agree that hypocrisy is a mark of pure evil.

"I AM SPARTACUS!"

Given the word's origin in Greek drama, it's always odd to hear practitioners of the dramatic arts damn people as hypocrites. If there's anyone who should understand the importance of playing a role, it's an actor.

One oft-voiced criticism of actors who involve themselves in causes or speak up about politics is that they're just acting. Asner's statement about people paying a price for speaking up is demonstrably far off the mark. Sean Penn, Tim Robbins, and Susan Sarandon regularly opine about the horrible things that we're doing to the environment or the evils of Republican rule or the ravages of AIDS, and they're Hollywood royalty.

The three are not unique in their habit of speaking clichés to power. Actors, directors, and the more visible members of the film and television industry regularly pronounce on every issue under the sun. Unfortunately, much of what they have to say is influenced by what I've decided to call the ghost of Hollywood past.

In this time when freedom of expression is only minimally restricted, actors and directors continue to be drawn to the blacklist, the old Hays Code,[20] and the dreaded studio system. Writer Dalton Trumbo was on an *actual blacklist* so it was understandable when he inserted the stand-up-and-be-counted "I am Spartacus!" ending to his Oscar-winning 1960 movie, but that idea has been replicated so often that it's grown tiresome.

In *Dead Poets Society* (1989), the students of an uptight boys school send off a beloved, happening teacher (played by Robin Williams) with a potentially expellable show of support, by standing on their desks and repeating, "O captain, my captain!" That was pushing it, but I have it on good authority that at a screening for movie critics of the Kevin Kline 1997 film *In & Out*, during the Big Gay Moment (with everybody announcing their fake homosexuality), one of the critics cut up the room by yelling, "I am Spartacus!"

Jim Carrey's 2001 commercial dud *The Majestic* was about a funny-guy writer who lost his memory, was adopted by a bunch of folks from small-town America, and eventually found himself before a committee that resembled the House Un-American Activities Committee. He refused to rat out his friends and won the public relations battle by showing them to be a bunch of humorless bureaucrats. At the time of its release, it was regarded as a project that Carrey had taken on to try to win an Oscar.

More recently, actor/director George Clooney decided to have a run at the former Wisconsin senator Joseph McCarthy in the Oscar-nominated movie *Good Night, and Good Luck*. Clooney's most interesting choice was not to hire an actor to play the part of McCarthy. Instead, he spliced in footage of Tail Gunner Joe from old newsreels to give the movie an in-the-moment feel.

It's a moment that many creative types are stuck in. You can see this in movies such as *Citizen Cohn* (1992), *The Front* ('76), *Concealed Enemies* ('84), and *Guilt by Suspicion* ('91), or you can ask a random celebrity for her opinion of U.S. politics and stand back. At the end of the screed, you might think that old Joe is still alive and raging, that all entertainment is still required to have a morally satisfactory ending, and that studios can buy and sell talent like used Chevys.

This in an era when every third actor owns her own production company, when studios send representatives to independent film festivals to pay decent money for promising films, and when DVD distribution promises to make the old movie theater rating system increasingly irrelevant.

Listen closely to these folks when they talk about the state of America today at rallies or on talk shows. Odds are, you'll hear the ghost of Hollywood past echoed in their words. Our liberties are constantly being trampled, our speech hushed up. There is a vicious struggle between us the sensitive creative few and the vast forces of intolerance and repression . . . who also happen to be our audience.

The ghost has suggested to them that the sort of people who go to see movies are fine, in their place, but give them an inch and censorship will descend on the country like a meteor. The impact would set us back to the bad old 1950s.

Because of this fear, discussion and cinematic portrayals of hot-button issues tend to be framed in terms of hypocritical repression and nonhypocritical freedom of expression (see *Pleasantville*, for instance). The hypocrite is a stock, two-dimensional character that's trotted out whenever the Who's Who want to write somebody out of polite society.

SOCRATIC METHOD ACTORS

It's disappointing that the Asners, Streisands, and Cusacks of the world often reach for easy villains. They might at least bring a more nuanced understanding of hypocrisy to the discussion. After all, they have access to special insights about hypocrisy, or should.

Every year, Hollywood gives us plenty of flat, uninteresting hypocrites, just as it draws on its own inexhaustible storehouse of jilted lovers and hookers with hearts of gold. But it also gives us more interesting hypocritical characters. They are, in fact, some of the more memorable characters in all of film.

We'll get to several of those characters, but I want to linger on this point for a brief moment. Why, if many actors are perfectly capable of portraying hypocrites with depth and rigor, do they then return to antihypocritical form the minute they step off of the stage? Why doesn't that experience translate into some sympathy for the bedeviled?

That old kidder Socrates nailed it when he said that poets and artisans have special inspiration but that they aren't good at understanding that inspiration. Their talent may well be "from the gods," he supposed, but it's hit and miss, and they can't explain why it hits. And so, like everybody else, they know nothing.

As you can imagine, the poets were none too happy about that judgment and they didn't take the criticism well. One of the three witnesses who helped to win a conviction against Socrates for corrupting the youth and disrespecting the gods was Meletus, a poet of some standing who didn't like being called a know-nothing.

With actors, the distinction should be made between intuitive knowledge and explicit knowledge. Intuitive knowledge is information that you have and use without thinking about it or necessarily understanding it. You *just know* something through repetition or through some strange quirk of existence. Both types of knowledge can be observed, on a sliding scale, in all kinds of human behavior.

The basic rules of tennis, for instance, are simple enough for any intelligent person to grasp. Most healthy, coordinated people can be taught how to play the game because the rules and normal play fall under the category of explicit knowledge. That is, they are fairly easily known and related to others. But knowledge of how to play tennis with a high level of skill comes from hitting and returning an awful lot of those fuzzy lime green balls and also from a natural sense that you either have or you don't.

Old tennis professionals earn a lot of money by teaching

young up-and-comers how to be great, but according to former pro and analyst Vic Braden, their explanations, not just for why they do certain things but even *how*, don't always square with their actions. He knows this because cutting-edge technology told him that he was being misled by many of the answers that he received.

According to the *New Yorker*'s resident best-selling contrarian Malcolm Gladwell, Braden turned match footage of several tennis pros into digitized, skeletal images and walked through these frame-by-frame. He paid particular attention to the position of their wrists during forehand shots. He did this because it was an article of faith among most pros that they use their wrist to roll the ball over the racket when they hit such a shot. Braden found that their explanation was wrong. That is, the tennis pros do often roll their wrists, but they do so *after* they've hit the ball, when it no longer makes any difference.

They roll their wrists because that's what a generation of former tennis pro coaches taught them to do, to put some extra oomph behind the ball. They hold off in doing so because some part of their natural genius for the game says, "Oh no you don't." And they misrepresent this to people because it all happens so fast that they don't consciously know what just happened.[21]

Actors are blessed (or cursed) with a similar problem as tennis players. Great performers have the ability to step into a role and *become* that person. They take on a different set of mannerisms and facial expressions and verbal tics. Their whole outlook, while in character, is different—often radically different.

A good actor "gets" what makes a character different and interesting and represents those traits to the audience. To ask him to explain that knowledge, let alone extrapolate lessons from it, reveals a flawed set of expectations. The actor's genius lies not in the explanation but in the, well, the . . .

ACTION!

Take Claude Rains, the English-born actor whose efforts in the movie *Casablanca* created an immortal fictional character. The film is rated near the top of lists of all-time best movies, including the American Film Institute's recent poll of 1,500 critics, actors, directors, and film industry professionals. It came in number two, losing out only to director Orson Welles's overrated box office flop, *Citizen Kane.*[22]

Casablanca took its name from a port city in the North African nation of Morocco that was governed by the French from 1912 into the 1950s. The movie is set during the early '40s, after France had fallen to Germany and before the United States had entered the war. The Nazis installed the puppet Vichy regime in France, but the French protectorates had slightly more independence. This wiggle room turned Casablanca into a way station for Europeans who wanted to get on to Lisbon and then to America.

Those who had money could purchase exit visas and those who didn't had to find a way to get them, either by thievery or by currying favor with sympathetic French officials. Enter Rains as Captain Louis Renault, the slight, smart, devious head of the local police department whose hypocrisy is legendary.

Enter also the Americans, former idealistic soldier of fortune turned drunkard nightclub owner Rick Blaine (played by

Humphrey Bogart) and his loyal black piano player Sam (Dooley Wilson). From stage right come a contingent of soldiers and officers of the Third Reich led by the loutish Major Strasser (Conrad Veidt). They are looking for a set of visas that bestow upon the owners absolute diplomatic immunity and also for a certain unofficial diplomat.

From stage left comes that diplomat, Victor Lazlo (Paul Henreid), leader of the European underground resistance. Lazlo is accompanied by his striking wife, Ilsa (Ingrid Bergman), the old flame who abandoned Rick in Paris as the Nazis were marching on the city. The literal stage on which most of the action occurs is Rick's Café, because, as Renault explains, "Everybody comes to Rick's."

"Everybody" includes the thief who killed a few Nazi functionaries to get at the supervisas. These get-out-of-town-free passes fall into Rick's possession, which sets up the conflicts that most critics tend to focus on: Between Rick's bitterness and his love for Ilsa. Between Ilsa's loyalty to her husband and her love for Rick. Between a selfish isolationism and a sacrificial, defiant idealism.

But the more interesting conflicts are to be found in Rains's portrayal of Captain Renault. Unlike Rick, he isn't an idealist who's been beat down by experience. Unlike Victor Lazlo, he isn't straightforward unless it suits. And he's not distracted by love or duty like Ilsa. Rather, he is power. He sets himself apart from the rest of the characters early on by announcing, "In Casablanca, I am master of my fate."

Captain Renault's corruption is beyond question. He demands bribes to turn a blind eye to illegal gambling. He will sign off on the exit visas of pretty but penniless female European émigrés if they're willing to sleep with him. (Police officer: "Excuse me Captain, another visa problem has come up." Renault: "Show her in.") He values order much more than justice, and he can be brutal.

In one of his more cold-blooded moments, Renault tells Victor Lazlo and wife that the visa thief was killed while in police custody. "I'm making out the report now," he explains. "We haven't quite decided whether he committed suicide or died trying to escape."

And yet, there is something that makes Renault different than the Nazis in quality, not just degree. The French official may want to placate Strasser, but in his conversations with the Germans, he doesn't give much ground. Strasser becomes annoyed by his frequent repetition of the word "third" in "Third Reich," so he inquires:

> **Strasser:** You repeat *Third* Reich as though you expected there to be others.
>
> **Renault:** Well, personally, Major, I will take what comes.

And when Strasser questions his loyalties, Renault professes not fealty to the Reich but a self-interested neutrality:

> **Strasser:** Captain, can we be entirely certain which side you are on?
>
> **Renault:** I have no conviction, if that's what you mean. I blow with the wind and the prevailing wind happens to be for Vichy.

Strasser: And if it should change?

Renault: Surely the Reich doesn't admit that possibility.[23]

But it becomes clear that Captain Renault does take sides. He sides with preserving certain manners and appearances, and he works to hold back darker impulses that would run riot through Casablanca under a less tolerant, less corrupt regime.

In one test case, Major Strasser wants Victor Lazlo arrested on the spot when he discovers him at Rick's, but Renault insists that the matter will be settled in a different way and in due course. When Lazlo asks if it is Renault's "order" that he come to police headquarters, the Captain replies, "Let us say it is my request. That is a much more pleasant word." He does not bow to initial German pressures to give them custody of Lazlo, an act that would have been in his own immediate interest.

Or take one of the most famous lines from the film. Captain Renault professes to be "shocked—shocked!—to find gambling going on in here," and uses the illegal roulette room as an excuse to shut Rick's down to placate the Nazis. It's memorable because of what comes next. The croupier hands him his winnings. Without missing a beat, Renault says, "Thank you very much," and yells, "Everybody out at once!"

The scene is often interpreted as a comical indictment of Renault's hypocrisy. Dr. Anton Kris said that while Strasser wanted Rick's shut down because of "vengeful motives," at least his "wickedness is not hypocrisy, because he does not wrap himself in goodness."

But Kris understates the gravity of the situation. The police captain had already tried to explain to Strasser that while his officers were "trying to cooperate with your government," it was quite another thing to "regulate the feelings of our people." That notion failed to take because Lazlo and company drowned out several Nazi soldiers singing "Die Wacht am Rhein" with a rousing performance of "La Marseillaise," with the help of Rick's house musicians.

Renault's ordering them out is part of the complicated, almost balletic, performance that Rains brings off brilliantly because he "gets" the really horrible situation that his character finds himself in. If the police captain doesn't at least pretend to accommodate the Nazis, he has no doubt what will come next, and that that would be a whole lot worse than the current genteel corruption.

His motives are complicated, as the French say, but Renault's sense of honor comes through in the end.

CHEAP SHOTS, INC.

Because *Hypocrisy* author Professor James Spiegel is interested in the intersection of culture and ideas, I asked for his favorite examples of hypocrites in film. He answered that movies contain "a lot of cheap shots, particularly in recent Hollywood films" that deal with religious characters.

Professor Spiegel allowed that it is "*always* easier to portray evil than genuine goodness." He gave a few examples of films that manage to pull this off—*Pulp Fiction* and *Les Miserables*—and admitted that, when you're dealing with religious themes, it is "hard to portray a kind of hypocrisy that isn't just a cheap shot."

One exception that he mentioned was Robert Duvall's 1997

movie *The Apostle*. He explained, "Duvall had to bankroll *The Apostle* himself. I think that most Hollywood moguls just couldn't stand the idea that a fundamentalist Pentecostal minister would be a sympathetic character. And on top of it all, he's the main character. He's the hero. 'No thank you,' right? But it works so well as a film because it's so true. It's authentic. In art you try to tell the truth. He was telling the truth and I guess Hollywood couldn't stand it."

Which isn't to say that Duvall's Sonny Dewey isn't a hypocrite. He's a Texas preacher who ends up running from the law after he publicly takes a baseball bat to a youth pastor because the younger man is sleeping with his wife. Sonny flees to backwater Louisiana where he takes a new name and repeatedly tries to seduce a married woman. He also starts a radio ministry and a bricks-and-mortar effort that does a lot of tangible good for people. He's extremely flawed and also extremely generous, and we see that he's become a better man in the end.

Spiegel is right that the portrayal of Sonny is positive, but the self-appointed "apostle" is not the only pastor to come through as a decent character in film. In fact, that used to be the usual order of things. Under the Hayes Code, portraying a pastor, priest, or rabbi in a negative light was extremely difficult, and religious ratings boards made it even harder. If filmmakers wanted to criticize clerics, they had to be crafty.

Witness the 1945 film *The Bells of St. Mary's*. In the classic directed by Leo McCarey, Father O'Malley's (Bing Crosby's) bottom-line mentality bumps up against Sister Benedict's (Ingrid Bergman's) gentle, stubborn determination, and she wins out in the end. The film affirmed the essential goodness of both characters because it had to. Mainstream movies were expected to respect the gods, including their designated representatives here on Earth.

It's easy to see how creative types would strain against those restrictions. And as the blacklist and the film codes eroded or were scrapped altogether, the portrayal of religious figures and religious practice became more unvarnished and negative. This opened up opportunities for serious drama, but it contributed greatly to conservative resentment of Hollywood.

Think of the baptism scene in *The Godfather* (1972). Director Francis Ford Coppola brilliantly set two events side by side and cut back and forth to make a point about the character of the new don. In the first, Michael Corleone (Al Pacino) becomes the godfather to his sister's baby. The church is ornate and most of what the priest has to say is in Latin. Corleone goes through the ritual of promising to help the child to be raised in the faith, and he publicly renounces evil. In the second, we see several coordinated hits that he has ordered, to snip loose ends, so to speak, before the Family relocates to Vegas.

It's a truly great scene not because it bashes religion but because it plumbs the depths of just how two-sided Corleone can be. It shows him affirming the highest form of goodness that he knows at the same time as his right-hand men are coldly murdering his rivals. It says something very true about human nature, and it would not have been able to get past the censors to a mass audience in the 1950s.

Recent movies have taken three different approaches to portraying religious figures. In the minority, you have basically decent if flawed pastors, like Sonny in *The Apostle*, Robert

DeNiro's character in *True Confessions* (1981), and the sympathetic chaplain in *Rudy* ('93). Then there's the caricature of the bad pastor, the stone killer in vestments. This sort of portrayal goes back to movies such as *The Manchurian Candidate* ('62) and the decidedly nonmainstream *Night of the Hunter* ('55), and continues with films like 2005's *Sin City*.

And don't forget the preacher as fraud. A pioneer in this genre was the 1960 film *Elmer Gantry* (1960). More contemporary mutations include movies like *The Exorcist* ('73) and my all-time favorite film starring Steve Martin.

MOCKINGBIRD

The curious thing about fraudulent preacher movies is that while they showcase the character of the cleric with unflattering klieg lighting, the films also affirm the standard Christian take on hypocrisy. The preachers are bad not because of their preaching but because they mock religious truths and basic morality.

Take Martin's 1992 effort *Leap of Faith*. At the film's opening, the camera focuses on the heat. It rises off of the highway in waves, distorting the view of the long, flat Kansas plains. The sun-baked surrounding consists of sparse vegetation and grass burnt light brown.

A caravan of buses and semi-trucks enters this barren land, and a run-in with a traffic cop introduces us to the characters along for the ride. Martin plays Jonas Nightingale, a traveling revivalist preacher who believes in one Supreme Being: himself. He risks a night in jail to get out of a speeding ticket, and the crew on the bus place bets on how it's going to turn out.

Using a series of quick "reads" that are the common tricks of magicians and psychics, Jonas guesses that the officer is (a) divorced and (b) alienated from his daughter and passes this off as divine revelation. He reduces the cop to tears and walks away with a donation to his "ministry." Then he makes those who bet against him eat a little crow. "Just say, 'Thank ya, Jesus!'" he mocks.

And then comes a further complication. One of the semis overheats, and the whole crew detours to the farming town of Rustwater. A part for the truck will take several days to arrive in this drought-stricken place, and the ringleader is told that they don't have a choice. The traveling circus will have to take a few days off.

But Jonas has a different idea: "I always have a choice. Set up. We'll play here." He prevails over the groans of his crew and the objection of the local sheriff. Will Braverman (Liam Neeson) insists that Rustwater "can't afford a revival."

What follows is one of the best examinations of hypocrisy ever filmed. You have Jonas, the con artist preacher who has latched on to religion for the money and for the challenge of convincing people to give it up willingly. His crew of miscreants work to help scam the audience. They feed Jonas information that he can announce as visions, they plant money in people's wallets to create the appearance of miracles, and they help manipulate the crowd for the fake charismatic healing part of the show.

In the other corner, you have the sane unbelievers, Sheriff Braverman and a waitress that Jonas wants to sleep with named Marva (Lolita Davidovich). Marva calls him a "phony," and

Braverman cautions the people from Rustwater against giving away their money to this "dancing bear." The sheriff publicly exposes some of the seedier parts of Nightingale's past, including car theft and white-collar crime.

The audience's reaction helps to drive home Dr. Kris's point that we wear selective blinders when it comes to the obvious hypocrisy of leaders that we agree with. Nightingale knows how to play the sentiments of the crowd like a violin. In Rustwater, he celebrates old-fashioned small-town virtues and simple piety while he raps riches, fast city life, and that high-church religion. He does an effective job selling himself as one of them. Because of this relationship, Jonas can respond to the sheriff's challenge by embracing the criticism.

"I grew up mistreated, so I lied and I cheated," Jonas explains. His petty crimes led to time in jail, and he has struggled to put that part of his life behind him. But his wanton past was worth it because while he was lying "face down in the gutter," he stared straight up "into the face of God" and found redemption. That experience is precisely what makes him the person that the people of Rustwater need to hear from.

"If you want to give up womanizing," he asks, "who are you going to talk to? Some pale-skinned virgin priest?"[24] Or that formerly wild and crazy guy, Jonas Nightingale?

VAPORS AND VIRTUES

In Renault and Nightingale, movie watchers can see two different types of hypocrite. The French police captain is not perfect, but he is close to the justified hypocrite. His double-dealing behavior often serves a higher purpose than his own short-term benefit. He finds himself in an intolerable situation, and his hypocrisy helps him to rise above it.

Nightingale is closer to the image that most people have in mind when they conjure up a hypocrite. He professes something that he doesn't believe in order to exploit the faith and goodwill of others. He preaches hope even though his own convictions are more of the "abandon all hope" persuasion.

During a crisis of faith, Nightingale preaches an anti-Sermon on the Mount to an empty revival tent. He begins by looking up at a crucifix and saying, "Hey, boss, remember me? Jack Newton. I've got a question for ya. Why'd you make so many suckers?"

Then he gets down to business: "You say love never endeth but I say love never starteth." The poor, the meek, the suffering are fated for more poverty, more humiliation, more pain. The smart bet is to check your hope at the door. But, of course, that message would have emptied the revival tent faster than Captain Renault blowing his whistle and yelling, "Everybody out!"

Both movies demonstrate a few enduring truths about hypocrisy. The first truth is that its traditional defenders are only half right to call it the price that vice pays to virtue. That's definitely true of Nightingale. He cynically professes belief in vapors and virtues that he doesn't believe in, but it is those things that he claims are for "suckers" that end up being true.

The more precise way of saying this is that hypocrisy helps to promote the good, so the transaction can go both ways. When the good is more or less rightly understood, as in Rustwater, it's the price that vice pays to virtue. When the usual norms are inverted, as in Casablanca, it's the price virtue pays to vice.

The second truth is that hypocrisy is everywhere, even if it is not always called by name. It is woven into the behavior of societies and affects nearly everyone: the preacher, the police officer, the city counselor, the barber, the milkmaid. It isn't recognized because it is sneaky. It hides behind justifications and weasel words and the universal desire to see ourselves as basically good people.

In fact, it usually operates so seamlessly that you might think it's some kind of law, like gravity or "market forces." You notice those things when people point them out, but usually they fade into the background. Sometimes the best place to hide is right in front of people's noses.

6

HIDDEN HYPOCRISIES

Emerson was right. A foolish consistency is the hobgoblin of small minds.

JONATHAN RAUCH

I first heard Jonathan Rauch speak at an event in Crystal City, Virginia, in late 2002. He delivered a keynote address at a journalism seminar put on by the Institute for Humane Studies. The subject of his talk was the importance of failure.

Rauch argued a lot of things that night, but he managed to lodge one vivid image in my head. He explained that capitalism is better than the alternatives not because it is stronger but because it tolerates weakness. It allows companies to fail, and gives the workers and management a chance to do something else.

The illustration came when he used the example of smoke-belching Soviet factories that actually subtracted value from the raw materials used to make consumer goods and other products. What came off the end of the factory line was worth less than the materials that were cut down, picked, or dug out of the ground.

The Politburo had sought to modernize the USSR by calling these factories into existence in the '40s and '50s. They put a scare in the West with what looked like impressive economic growth. This reported success led some thinkers to play up the virtues of central planning and to warn that America and Co. would fall behind unless we changed. Eliminate unnecessary competition and you could focus on production, production, production and really give the Commies a run for their money.

But once the Soviet Union fell, these factories became irrefutable evidence that you can have too much of even a good thing. Production was set by a central authority rather than the demands of the people, so Soviet factories produced either too many goods that people didn't want or not nearly enough of things they really needed.

Shortages became common and Russians got used to standing in lines to get what they could. Over time, the output of the factories slumped. Because they couldn't go broke, because the central planners dared not shut them down, bureaucratic mandates got in the way of useful output.

The normal industrial innovation that happened in much of the rest of the world passed the Soviet factories by. Rauch said that some of the factories were indeed cutting edge—fifty years ago. But the conditions that would normally prod people to try new things just weren't there. If creativity is punished, as it often was, then why try new things, especially if they get in the way of temporary production goals? That could land the would-be innovator in the gulag.

By creating a system that was too big to fail, Russian rulers had guaranteed that their subjects could not really succeed. It slowed and stifled them. It tried to substitute planning for judgment. And that, more than any diplomatic pressure, eventually caused the regime to fall over like a stack of over-produced dominoes.

Rauch then applied the lessons from the Soviet factories to an unlikely subject: himself. He took the audience through his career as a journalist and scholar and stressed the importance of taking chances and never getting too comfortable with what we are doing right now.

It had to rank as one of the oddest motivational speeches of all time. He capped it off by telling us to go forth and boldly fail.

RAUCH-COLORED GLASSES

Rauch is a scholar at the Brookings Institution, a venerable center-left think tank that Nixon administration hatchet man Chuck Colson wanted to firebomb for its role in the publication of the Pentagon Papers.[1] He writes a column every other week for the influential policy magazine *National Journal,* and he's won a National Magazine Award in the "columns and commentary" category, a recognition that is probably more coveted than a Pulitzer.

The *National Journal* column is a must-read in D.C. because Rauch is both a high-concept thinker and a detail man. He sees the world of ideas and the world of, say, hot dogs, as one and the same. He is able to look at the same things that many other people observe but see them very differently, and then make others see through his thin wire-rimmed glasses.

I wanted to borrow his lenses to help me better understand

why there is so much hypocrisy and so much hatred of hypocrisy. Why, I wondered, do we behave so inconsistently and self-servingly but then denounce those traits in others? Why are people so often fooled by hypocrites? Is it just fear of uncertainty and wishful thinking, as Dr. Anton Kris says, or is there something more?

Rauch spoke with me in the fall of 2005 to flesh out a notion that he has labeled "Hidden Law." Normally, you think of law as something written down in books and enforced by civil or other authorities, but that isn't the only way to understand all the rules that we live by, and are measured against.[2]

So what is Hidden Law? It is a series of "tacit rules," said Rauch—a bunch of "expected norms and behaviors and rewards and punishments, none of which are encoded formally any-where" that govern our behavior. Hidden Law is the sum total of all the unwritten rules that we "rely on to work out day-to-day problems and conflicts." One vulgar synonym might be "customs," but that fails to convey the full meaning of what Rauch is driving at.

Here are a few examples of Hidden Law in practice:

- It is considered poor form to strike a child. But if a parent cuffs his screaming kid in public or yanks him away to administer a more private, more painful lesson, most folks avert their gaze and pretend nothing's happening.

- In baseball, if a pitcher from the Seattle Mariners beans a batter from the Oakland Athletics, there is—how to say this?—a very high probability that an A's pitcher will brush back a Mariner with an inside pitch in the next inning.

- If you shoot a cop, chances are you won't live to surrender to police custody, and if you do, you'll likely have to spend some time in the hospital to recover from the bullet wound. Most people know this, and it makes them wary of pulling the trigger when a police officer is on the other end of the barrel.

All of these examples involve violations of written-down laws or regulations. And yet these actions are widely, though not universally, accepted as being the way that things work. As long as you aren't a stickler for doing everything by the book, these so-called "exceptions to the rule" probably make sense to you at a visceral level.

Of course we should give parents discretion in disciplining their children. They know better than we do how to make their children behave decently. In the lion's share of cases, the mother or father's affection and sense of responsibility for their children will stop them from inflicting lasting harm.

So what if the umpire looks the other way or only issues a halfhearted warning? There really are such things as control issues and if they tossed pitchers out for pitching inside, the teams would have to expand their rosters. Besides, the tit-for-tat can help to keep the pitchers honest. If they bean someone on the other team, one of their own teammates is likely to be awfully sore at them.

And *what is with* the exquisite concern for cop killers? Yes, police officers ignore normal protocols when dealing with people who take a shot at their fellow officers. So what? They're in a dangerous line of work as it is. It would be even more dangerous if people thought they could fire at cops without facing return fire.

LITTLE GREEN OBSERVERS

Those explanations may sound superficially reasonable, but pure reason has little to do with it. Rauch calls Hidden Law "pre-rational." If you think that these actions are OK in some specific instances, it's not going to be because you would approve of them in the abstract.

If another parent were to seize your hypothetical child in a supermarket, give him a swat, and tell him to shut up, you'd be upset. You might call security. If you were inventing baseball from scratch, you probably wouldn't be cruel enough to invent the "fair play or you pay" rule. And I don't think that I'm going out on a limb to say that you would not give police the right to put a bullet in someone who wanted to turn himself in.

We tend to wink at these things because of accumulated experience. Rauch argued that Hidden Law is like "popular knowledge" because it's "evolutionary. It operates quietly, usually, and it evolves as it goes along. And often it appears not to make any sense if you come in from the outside and look at it."

Imagine outsiders—say, Martians—trying to understand American modes of behavior, and you can begin to understand how odd Hidden Law really is. It's unwritten and usually unspoken. It often goes against laws or principles that we claim to revere.

The Martians would be pulling their little green hair out trying to understand it, at first. But over time they might find, with Rauch, that beneath the chaos there is a "seamless web" of unwritten rules that work well. Outsiders would also observe subtle changes over time that people who are under its spell might not notice. Rauch explained how Hidden Law changes by giving the example of public schools of thirty or forty years ago.

"Principals, assistant principals especially, used to have a lot of discretion to smack a kid if he was misbehaving," he said. "Most assistant principals understood that if they hit a kid [in a way] that would hurt or bruise that kid, if there was a hospital or doctor visit as a result of that, that that [meant] serious trouble." Such an action might "lead to a parent complaining," and the junior bureaucrat "knew that it violated the norm," and so he would pull his punches, literally.

These largely unspoken understandings, said Rauch, produced "regimes in schools, including the public school where I went . . . where there were actually very few, comparatively few really severe excesses." This restraint was possible because "most of the people knew where the limits were."

Rauch said that the gradual adjustments of Hidden Law have to do with those limits. The unwritten code of conduct can be "self-correcting, because people will debate it. If something goes far enough, it will and should prick people's consciences and they will say the norm here is absolutely wrong . . . and Hidden Law will change. I think that it is in some ways more adaptive to moral reasoning than public law is."

If it sounds far-fetched that an unwritten set of rules can act as an effective restraint, then consider that Brits frequently refer to their "constitution" that doesn't, technically, exist, but that has helped to safeguard British liberties for hundreds of years. And English Common Law is based on precedents rather than statute, and evolves over time.

Common Law theoretically gives judges an awful lot of power to change rules and legislate from the bench. And yet judges in that tradition have tended to be a lot less expansive in their findings than judges who work within legal traditions that claim to adhere only to statutory law. In America, the Supreme Court has upended social mores and radically reshaped society. In Britain, that job has usually fallen to Parliament.

The reason for their judicial reserve is the sensitivity of Common Law judges to tacit agreements and unwritten rules. Their legitimacy depends upon arrangements that aren't much more explicit, and so the judges tend to pay closer attention, and they try not to thrash around like a bull in an antique store.

FIRST RULE OF FIGHT CLUB

Rauch expressed some skepticism about his use of public schools to vindicate Hidden Law ("I have filibustered you there"), but I decided that he had accidentally found an interpretive key to rival the Rosetta Stone.

It may be hard to remember this, but public schools used to work. The overall performance was better. Order could be kept. Schools in poor areas were not necessarily mired in poor management, drugs, and violence. A good part of what made schools work was a set of tacit agreements that are not tolerated today.

The teachers and administrators had authority because they were allowed to mete out punishment to students and engage in other activities that we would not tolerate today. Parents, to a great extent, understood that that was what it took to manage unruly children. The principal of one of the elementary schools that I attended told the story of his dad matching the school principal swat for swat if he learned that his son had misbehaved.

The days of corporal punishment in public schools are largely behind us, and the switch isn't the only thing that's vanished. It used to be that unruly kids could be easily expelled, but there were also other, informal ways of dealing with disturbances and violence.

You've probably heard of a teacher who would chuck chalkboard erasers at kids who fell asleep in class, but ask people who were educated in the 1960s or earlier what tended to happen when two young men started to exchange blows. You might be surprised to learn that a good number of people have some variation of the following story:

Two boys were arguing in the hallway and one pushed the other up against a locker. He threw a clumsy uppercut and then a teacher caught them both by surprise. The teacher grabbed them by their shirts and dragged them outside of school and told the boys that they were going to have it out here and now. He instructed: no scratching, no kicking, no hitting below the belt. Go.

The teacher let them throw punches for a few minutes while a crowd of students looked on. Every time one boy seemed to have the advantage, he broke them up, let the other get his bearings, and then let them have at it again. When they were both bruised and tired, he said, "That's enough." He made them shake hands and agree to let that be the end of the conflict, and it usually was.

If that sort of thing were to happen in a public school now, the teacher would be suspended and then fired and possibly face criminal charges. And it's almost a foregone conclusion that the school would be sued over negligence for allowing a hostile environment.

But it wouldn't get that far because the previous remedy is no longer an option. Instead, most public schools have a regime of zero tolerance. Fisticuffs still occur, but the students have it out away from the eyes of teachers and principals. The authorities no longer tacitly sanction the violence, and they're no longer there to referee and guarantee that it doesn't spiral out of control.

The end of refereed fights may be a little thing, but it's part of a larger problem of discipline in schools. Teachers are afraid to lay a hand on children for fear of lawsuits, so they send them to principals who are likewise tied down by rules and threats of litigation. And those administrators face an impossible problem: If they suspend or expel students, the parents will probably sue. And if they don't act and the student does something heinous, that also opens the school up to liability.

That uncertainty leads to some particularly mockable outcomes. In order to shore up their legal position in more serious cases, schools are forced to pass and rigorously enforce rules that are the stuff of ridiculous headlines.

When little Jason gets sent home for pretending that his finger is a gun, we are rightly outraged. However, what we don't realize is that those cases are not wholly irrational. To make the case against the real offenders, schools have adopted the strategy of making life more unpleasant for everybody.

And when parents come knocking on school administrators' doors to complain that their children were sent home for silly reasons, they are frequently told that rules are rules. End of discussion.

"Zero tolerance is just a way of saying no exceptions and no exceptions is just a way of saying we're going to treat anybody absolutely the same all the time and we won't have discretion," said Rauch.

Many parents put it even more pithily:

zero tolerance = zero sense.

KNOW YOUR RIGHTS

Not so fast, said G. Robb Cooper when I spoke to him early in 2006: "Zero tolerance doesn't mean zero discretion."[3]

Cooper speaks from experience. He is a partner in the law firm Ottosen, Britz, Kelly, Cooper & Gilbert and a pioneer in education law. He was a teacher and then a school principal who wanted to become a superintendent. When Cooper went back to school to get his Ph.D., he decided to earn a law degree at the same time. At the end of which, "To be blunt, I was made an offer I couldn't refuse." He decided to practice law.

As a lawyer for school districts in Illinois and all over the country, his job is to fire bad or abusive teachers and to help expel problem students. Public schools need lawyers like Cooper in order to function because of the regime of rights that has become increasingly important over the last thirty-odd years.

"When people started using the term *zero tolerance* it was a popular catchphrase," Cooper explained, "especially in the Reagan years. You know, 'zero tolerance.' We're not going to put up with this kind of behavior anymore."

Laws and rules were enacted to help cut down on violence, drug use, and other societal ills, and these measures were cheered, especially in inner city schools, where discipline had totally broken down. But some have charged that the rules were too rigidly and stupidly enforced. Complaints led to news stories that made school districts the butts of many jokes.

I asked Cooper about this phenomenon. Specifically, I said, "Headlines regularly tell us that students are sent home for really ridiculous reasons, including pointing a one-quarter-inch G. I. Joe gun at other students and saying, 'Bang!'" And I wondered: "Hasn't this gotten a bit out of hand?"

"My experience, because I represent school boards, is that that's never the full story," he explained. "And we're not going to give them the full story because students have privacy rights."

But Cooper could say that suspensions for scenarios similar to the one I spelled out are "often punishments for other actions as well. There have been a series of behavioral problems and then the principal says, 'OK, that's the last straw.'"

It's true, he said, that "we won't tolerate weapons, racial slurs, or violence, but that doesn't mean that people get the same punishment. We always handle each student discipline matter on a case-by-case basis."

He continued, "Both federal law and Illinois law outlaw weapons in school. That doesn't mean that a child who brings a knife to school to help cut his lunch will receive the same punishment as the one who brings a gun. People make a lot of the fact that if a child brings a weapon to school, then by our statute, we must expel him for a year. But they don't read the whole statute."

The full statute allows that both the school board and the superintendent may modify a punishment to take the facts on the ground into account. Parents can insist on a review of their child's punishment by different layers of school authority. And if that fails, there are always court proceedings that they can initiate.

As for how often that occurs, Cooper didn't have "good empirical data," but he did have a few impressions from twenty years of dealing with problem cases.

"What I'm seeing now is, it's kind of come back full circle. It used to be that students and parents fought everything and then a new crop of students was more subdued. Now, I've observed parents challenging schools on nearly every act of discipline. I recently had a case where the parent insisted on going all the way to a full hearing over a one-day in-school suspension. It was ridiculous."

It's also a great way of providing employment for lawyers. When he was talking about parents taking it to the mattresses all the time, Cooper quipped, "My banker loves that." The city of Chicago, he said, employs about ten in-house attorneys. For my own hometown of Lynden, Washington (population: 10,000, give or take[4]), he estimated the school district sets aside $30,000 to $40,000 every year for legal fees.

Cooper went into education law because (a) he believes deeply in public education, and (b) he saw a genuine need for lawyers to help the schools function. And he's had some success in removing substantial roadblocks to learning. At one point in our conversation, he let on that he may have been responsible for firing a particularly horrible teacher from my middle school.

What I wanted to know was this: what if the law itself is functioning as a roadblock? I asked, has the increased focus on rights and process actually produced "any good" as far as educating students is concerned?

"There's been a realization that the organization has to be responsive to the law and we can't trample rights," he said. "When I was in school, administrators were obsessed with hair length, skirt length, whether people were wearing collared shirts. Those are stupid things that detract from what we should be interested in."

And: "When you look at tenure rights for public school teachers, it's to protect them against the arbitrary and capricious acts of boards of education. We don't want local school board members coming after teachers because they didn't play their son on the softball team.

"Has there been an overreaction? Maybe. But it's better now that students are not disciplined arbitrarily or capriciously," he said.

Cooper ended our conversation with a ringing endorsement

of democracy and the rule of law, which seemed an awful lot like ducking the question to me.

"TOO BAD FOR YOU"

But maybe it was just another way of looking at the question. Between Rauch and Cooper, you have a conflict of visions about how the world works. As a gay man who grew up in Arizona, Rauch is no fan of corporal punishment or trampling of minority rights. But when he looks at schools of the past, he can't help but notice that they functioned well with few of the safeguards that Cooper sees as absolutely necessary. Why?

When Rauch looks at the schools' success, he sees relatively few explicit rules supplemented by a good helping of Hidden Law. The teachers and administrators back then had a freer hand, but they were also more vulnerable to dismissal by school boards, which, in turn, were restrained by experience rather than by statute.

People of a certain cast of mind looked at that situation and saw a recipe for chaos. And so more and more "rights" were created. Teachers were granted a property right to tenure, often after very few years on the job. Students were given a number of rights against teachers and principals. And then school districts had to bring in lawyers like Cooper just to make the system workable. It may have been a victory for democracy and the rule of law, but as for as the quality of classroom education . . . not so much.

The problem, said Rauch, is "this intensely bureaucratic mindset, which believes in one transparent rule. Transparent, fair, equal, predictable rules set down in advance, with a minimum of quote-unquote loopholes. Process over all." He calls this approach an "ideology" and labels that ideology "Bureaucratic Legalism."

He argues that Bureaucratic Legalism is like Kryptonite to Hidden Law because, as resilient as they may be in other circumstances, tacit arrangements usually yield to explicit ones. It's not like you can enforce understandings in court the way that you can enforce statutory laws or contracts. And since we've decided to settle these things in court, that pretty much finishes off Hidden Law as a going concern.

By embracing Bureaucratic Legalism, Rauch warned, schools have "set in place a motion that will, over time, attempt to iron out all quote-unquote inconsistencies, reduce the role of local, spontaneous judgment, reduce the role of situational context, all on the grounds of making everything perfectly fair and knowable in advance."

"Lawyers," he explained, "just hate inconsistency. They think it's wrong and want to stamp it out whenever they see it. But Emerson was right. A foolish consistency is the hobgoblin of small minds."

The *National Journal* scribe told me that he first became interested in the conflict between these two visions in the early '90s, when he was looking at speech codes on college campuses. These new campus codes spelled out what people could say in advance and specified penalties for offensive speech by students. Those who said un-PC things found themselves hauled before campus tribunals and publicly berated for their insensitivity.

Speech codes, Rauch decided, "were another good example

of Bureaucratic Legalism going where the law had no business at all. The old gentlemen's codes did a much better job of dealing with bad conduct on campus."

According to the gentlemen's codes, the rule was, first, "don't act like a cad." Failing that, "If you do act like a cad, pretend that you were drunk at the time and apologize the next day." And if you failed to apologize, "the dean can throw you out and that's tough shit. Or, if you pop off once too often and somebody slugs you in the nose, too bad for you. You've learned your lesson."

Rauch called the older way of doing things "very flexible, very intuitive. It worked extremely well" in allowing a relatively free exchange of ideas while enforcing basic manners. He argues that it worked because it allowed the rough and tumble of private judgment to stand in the place of uniform public rules.

THE RIGHT TO HYPOCRISY

Much of Hidden Law wouldn't be possible without hypocrisy. Unspoken rules work to regulate all kinds of behavior, from the very public to what Rauch calls those "deep, subterranean moral issues" that nobody really wants to talk about. Like sex and adultery.

"Decent hypocrisy," Rauch explained, is "an extremely important part of Hidden Law in [the] more narrow sense, the sense of that part of Hidden Law which is so hidden that we don't even acknowledge it exists, and we deny it's going on. We pretend nothing is happening at all.

"That absolutely depends on hypocrisy. It not only depends

upon genteel hypocrisy, which is the preacher pretending not to be screwing the congregant, it depends on public hypocrisy, which is people actually averting their eyes.

"If the preacher is playing his part by pretending not to be screwing the congregant—you know, checking into motels on the far edge of town under a pseudonym—then that imposes a further hypocritical burden on the rest of us to pretend we don't know what's going on. . . .

"Decent hypocrisy, as it's been called in different contexts, comes in for a lot of ridicule because at one level it's absolutely absurd. Because you've got all these people who know about this bad stuff going on, who are probably gossiping to each other about this bad stuff, yet who, somehow, in public, manage to deny it or act as if it's not even going on. They all manage to pretend they're averting their gaze."

That hypocritical arrangement is not, Rauch cautioned, a blank check for just any old kind of behavior. If the man is too flagrant or if his wife decides to call him out publicly, then people are reliably shocked—shocked!—to find out what has been going on. The people's hypocrisy in that case isn't ideal, but it's probably less bad than the alternative of busting up a marriage and condemning the children to every other weekend with daddy.

Rauch also brought up the case of a church wedding in which the bride was visibly knocked up. It ran against the normal rules to allow such a ceremony, but, incredibly, "an entire congregation pretended not to see that the bride was pregnant at the wedding. Obviously, they all knew. Obviously, they all gossiped about it behind their hands. But, publicly, she was getting married. She was doing the right thing: 'I don't see anything, do you?'"

That outcome depended on "not just hypocrisy but many layers of hypocrisy and it required a number of different hypocrites to play their separate roles and do so in concert." And they worked to produce the best possible result under the circumstances.

He gave one other example that's relevant here. In the gay community, the debate about outing closeted homosexuals can be particularly fierce. To the question, "When is a person's sexual orientation fair game for publication?" the standard answer has been openly gay Representative Barney Frank's position that "the right to privacy does not entail the right to hypocrisy"—but Rauch disagrees.

"That's wrong because the right to privacy depends on the right to hypocrisy. People do stuff in private that we don't want to know about. Because if we knew about it we might have to legislate to stop it," he said.

He explained by contrasting the "Michael Kinsley view of the world" with the "Main Street view of the world." Kinsley, Bill Bennett's erstwhile persecutor, "who's a brilliant writer, delights in exposing hypocrisy, and thinks every time he's done so he's scored an intellectual coup.

"It's a lot of fun to observe this, but ultimately I think it misses the whole point, which is that much of what goes on in public life"—even things that concern those "deep subterranean moral issues"—"depends on a certain amount of hypocrisy."

And when that unspoken hypocritical consensus is challenged, the results can be a kind of train wreck.

"I DID NOT HAVE SEX WITH THAT WOMAN"

Hidden Law usually yields to its opposite number, but what do you get if you take them both, fire them up, and run them down different ends of the same train tunnel?

You get the Clinton impeachment.

Chugging away in one direction was the Office of the Independent Counsel, which Rauch describes as the "all-time champion of Bureaucratic Legalism." The statute established a "self-financing, completely independent legal bureaucracy devoted to obsessively pursuing one allegation of possible misconduct no matter where it might lead or no matter what the cost."

Independent Counsel Kenneth Starr had been appointed for reasons that had nothing to do with sexual harassment.[5] But when former Arkansas state employee Paula Jones dragged the president into court over a pass that he'd made at her, Clinton's Lothario-like sexual history became fodder for Jones's lawyers.[6] And when the president dissembled under oath about having sex with a White House intern, charges of perjury hit the fan in late 1998.

Normally, congressional Republicans might have cut a president some slack. But Bill Clinton was a special case. He'd championed the Independent Counsel statute when he was running for office against George H. W. Bush and made a big show about signing the reauthorization bill. And he'd signed legislation that broadened discovery in sex harassment cases. You could make the argument that he had it coming.

In an elegant essay for the *New York Times*, novelist and lawyer Richard Dooling spelled out the dilemma that the House

Judiciary Committee faced. He asked, "At what point do the evils of intrusive, well-meaning laws outweigh their benefits?" His answer was "now," but he cautioned that it had better not be a one-off thing.

"Any male supervisor who has consensual sex with another employee in any American workplace could be sued and deposed in the way Mr. Clinton was. Thanks to ever-expanding theories about what constitutes harassment, even private, consensual sex is fair game for questioning. What if, instead of punishing women who decline his unwanted advances, a powerful male employer simply rewards women who do consent to have sex with him? Does that violate Title VII sexual harassment laws? Probably. Let's question him under oath about his sexual relationships and let the jury decide. If he lies about sex to protect his family, it's perjury," Dooling explained.

Congress should repeal the laws or remove the president from office, he argued. Otherwise, the Greek statesman Solon would have been proved right when he said, "Laws are like spiders' webs which, if anything small falls into them they ensnare it, but large things break through and escape."[7]

President Clinton didn't help his case when he went on national television to tell us that he "did not have sexual relations with that woman, Miss Lewinsky." Or when he replied to the "confirm or deny" questions put forward by the Judiciary Committee with the most mealymouthed hairsplitting I'd ever read. Or when he sicced the White House attack dogs on his opponents to paint them as a bunch of sex-obsessed voyeurs, and worse.

Even after having been drubbed in the '98 midterm elections,

House Republicans decided that the naked hypocrisy of this Democratic president was just too much, and that public opinion would eventually come around. They voted to impeach him and sent the case to the Senate for removal proceedings.

But they didn't count on the little engine that could. As with the campaign finance scandals, the mob saved Bill Clinton. Polls consistently showed that people were dead set against removing him from office. Americans would toy with the idea that a president could be removed from office for perjuring himself about other matters, but they hypocritically put "lying about sex" into a different category, and refused to budge.

In this stubborn resistance to the president's removal, many conservatives saw moral rot, and complained loudly about it. Bennett's quickie anti-Clinton pamphlet *The Death of Outrage* climbed the best-seller lists as those few remaining outraged souls used their filthy lucre to demonstrate their solidarity, and, for what it's worth, I was one of them.

Rauch had a radically different interpretation of the public's stubbornness. He saw it as their embrace of the older ways over and against a scorched earth legal process that left no room for privacy or error.

President Clinton was married and his wife was standing by him. So the voters pretended to avert their eyes, even though they clearly knew better.

GOING DUTCH

Rauch saw the rejection of Clinton's impeachment as a sign that the public was starting to prefer the hypocrisy of Hidden Law to the consistency of Bureaucratic Legalism. But I'm not so sure either that he's right or, if so, that it would matter all that much.

In his defense, the Independent Counsel law was allowed to expire at the stroke of midnight on June 30, 1999, and few people are clamoring to bring it back. The collective memory is too vivid and painful. One of the few saving graces of the Bush years has been the absence of regular reports and speculations about what the latest Lawrence Walsh wannabe has uncovered.

On the other hand, once an entire political class was stung by a self-financed bureaucracy with nearly unlimited oversight powers, you'd think that nobody would ever propose such a silly idea ever again. But in the wake of the recent scandals kicked up by lobbyist Jack Abramoff, several congressmen have floated the idea of an independent commission to police Congress.[8]

Outside the realm of electoral politics and congressional reform issues, the prospects for contradiction look worse. Rauch admitted that rolling status quo "has tremendous self-generating momentum and it now has this huge bureaucratic establishment behind it, this entire infrastructure of lawyers whose job is to do Bureaucratic Legalism and to insinuate it in places that it has never gone before."

So even while Hidden Law can mark the occasional X in the untrumpeted "win" column, most of the important battles are won by the paper pushers without much of a struggle. We get more law and less judgment, more process and less discretion, and this has a serious effect on the broader culture.

The lawyers and bureaucrats are egged on by activists who assume that if a few laws and restrictions are a good thing, then more would be so much better. It reminds me of that that old

newspaper man H. L. Mencken's jab that democracy is based on
the theory that the people know what they want and deserve to
get it good and hard.

Their activities also bring to mind another image, of those
smoke-belching Soviet factories, stuck in the past, slowed by age
and stifled by bureaucracy, subtracting value from everything
they touch.

To wit, the issue of assisted suicide. Before the Supreme
Court's narrow decision to uphold Oregon's assisted suicide law,[9]
I asked Rauch what he thought about the efforts to allow doctors
to kill their patients.

He said that there was a "whole lot" to recommend the old
regime which "squared the circle by allowing assisted suicide as
long as it stayed out of sight and as long as it was never acknowledged, and as long as everyone involved pretended it wasn't going
on. You had an extremely private, extremely localized kind of
decision making involving doctors and relatives, immediate family members and the person themselves, and no suicide ever offi-
cially happened."

Rauch continued: "This is actually portrayed in the movie
The English Patient, and it used to be not at all uncommon. I
know personally of a friend of mine whose father committed
assisted suicide with the help of a doctor. Not a word was ever
spoken about it but everybody knew. And that was a good way
of preserving the commitment to life and human dignity without forcing a legal showdown.

"Once you get a legal showdown, it gets very hard not to
go bipolar—all or nothing—with immense numbers of prosecutors and public officials, judges and lawyers, second-guessing

every decision, and people getting into trouble when they're really trying to do the humane thing under extremely difficult circumstances."

In other words, we already had a de facto exception for assisted suicide, with certain hypocritical safeguards built in. It was illegal for doctors to kill patients, but they could wink, nod, and caution very strongly that one would not want to take too many of "these pills" or overdo it on the morphine drip.

When that happened, we all looked the other way. Family members kept mum, insurance companies signed off on it, prosecutors saw nothing out of place. It was unfortunate, it was tragic, and it was none of our business.

That wasn't enough for advocates of assisted suicide, who decided to make it our business. They weren't content with the ability to kill oneself quietly in those final, painful days. Jack Kevorkian and company also wanted recognition. They wanted to force society as a whole to confer its blessings on doctor-assisted killing and to change the way we think about suicide in the process.

The result, at press time, is that assisted suicide is now legal in the state of Oregon and illegal everywhere else, and the enhanced scrutiny is having unfortunate side effects. Coupled with the Drug Enforcement Agency's recent crackdown on doctors who overprescribe pain medication, the issue is doing yeoman's work to prolong the suffering of people who wanted nothing to do with the whole debate.

High fives all around.

7

I, HYPOCRITE

Oh Lord, please don't let me be misunderstood.

THE ANIMALS

If you have read this far and do not think better of hypocrisy than you did going in, then this book has failed. Given the subject matter, I don't think we can write this off as a noble effort. If hypocrisy is the unrelenting vice that most people believe it to be, then its defenders are, at best, deluded. If they are defending hypocrisy with a clear mind and an untroubled conscience, they are doing something morally reprehensible. You might let them go on out of a respect for free speech, but you have no obligation to take them seriously.

I hope that's not the case here. I hope these words have found some resonance with you, and that your mind is open to the possibility that the defendant is being set up. Speaking up for hypocrisy is not some demented attempt at contrariness for its own sake. It's an attempt at defending the defensible. So I ask the jurors to weigh the following words carefully.

Hypocrisy has been blamed for an awful lot of bad, but the

blame is ill-thought, mostly. When one is damned as a hypocrite, his hypocrisy is often the best thing about him, because it points in the right direction. Max Scheler was an ethicist and also a bit of a lech. He argued that the sign that shows the way to Boston doesn't have to go there in order to do something useful for the rest of us.

Scheler was right about that, I think. In societies that are reasonably non-screwed-up, the appearance that hypocrites put on is a good one. Their vices at least have the decency to clothe themselves with better notions. It is better to have the bad acknowledge the good and to publicly conform to the right than for it to operate with no restraints at all. We should prefer Jim Bakker to the garden-variety sociopath.

Hypocrites may be bad people, in the main. However, think twice before deploying that judgment. Most of us behave hypocritically at times. We can refuse to think of our behavior as such, but what does that change? Not much.

Brave New World author Aldous Huxley said it best: Facts do not cease to exist because they are ignored.[1] Hypocrisy does not cease to be hypocrisy if we rationalize it away or call it by another name. And moral weakness can be every bit the self-serving dodge to cover over a series of "lapses" that add up to full-blown hypocrisy.

Too many of those professed nonhypocrites adopt the "saint or shut up" approach, rejecting the moral standing of all save a canonized few for failure to live up to every jot and tittle of what they preach. Professor Spiegel's father's loud judgment ("Hypocrites! Lousy hypocrites!") is not just a way of avoiding an argument, it's also dumb.

The subtitle of this volume, "Picking Sides in the War on Virtue," gets at an interesting notion. Many of the standard, reflexive objections to hypocrisy are really objections to moral reasoning and moral improvement. The antihypocrite ends up being the anti-Jiminy Cricket, heckling any attempts at passing on moral lessons to others:

> Don't do drugs, kids.
> *What about that bowl you smoked in the seventh grade?*
> *Or your entire freshman year in college?*

> Don't sleep around.
> *Remember that stewardess at the convention in Topeka?*

> Don't drink so much.
> *Says the guy with the DUI in Ohio.*

> Don't steal.
> *Pack of gum, Safeway, 1985.*

> Don't cheat.
> *Oh please. College trig test. Give me a hard one.*

> Don't swear so much.
> *Remember last week when you dropped a hammer on your*
> *big toe? So does everybody else in a ten-block radius.*

Granted, Professor Spiegel has a point about the importance of humility. All moralists should be humble because, if we are honest, we know that we have much to be humble about.

But the modern antihypocritical stance leads to a lot of bad outcomes. It stifles and shuts up. It disrupts the normal processes of moral reasoning.

YOU BIG, NAKED APE

Other than, say, grooming habits, the things that separate men from animals are our intelligence and our moral faculty. We can learn much more than the beasts of the field and the air, and we can conceive of the good quite outside our own narrow interests and biological drives.

It's not an easy trick, of course, and moral progress is halting. Some problems are so thorny that they take generations to solve and, even then, the gains are not as sticky as one would like.

The twentieth century was supposed to be the pinnacle of cultural and scientific achievement, and in many ways it bore out the most optimistic predictions of starry-eyed futurists. But they didn't see that it would also be one long bloodbath. One failed ideology after the other tried to change human nature by culling the herd of undesirable traits. Man wouldn't change fast enough, so the true believers tried to manage him like an animal. They substituted selective breeding for moral struggle, and failed utterly.

You see, moral progress can only happen if people are free to consider what's right quite apart from whether their own actions are always good. Prophets, politicians, and pamphleteers try out statements of principle even if they don't immediately endorse the full implications of those statements, and even if their own behavior contradicts those principles, sometimes flagrantly. Over time, their ideas can work to change our interests and move us toward the good.

Moral wiggle room is needed in order for real progress to happen, and that wiggle room is provided by hypocrisy.

To wit, according to the modern canons of consistency, you can be a slaveholder or you can endorse the equality of all men, but not both. By the standards of today, that's true, but that hypocritical position was embraced by America's founders. Many of them owned slaves while they affirmed that all men were created equal, including that virtuoso of Enlightenment culture and drafter of the Declaration of Independence, Thomas Jefferson.

We can look back on their situation with a sneer, as many intellectuals have done, or we can learn from it. Much of the world is better off because the U.S. rebels endorsed the equal dignity of all men, even if they wanted to implement it unevenly and self-servingly. It was the principle of equality that led many of the founders to free their own slaves, if only on their deathbeds. And that principle led to the abolition of the dread institution, here and elsewhere.

Most people will agree that that was a great thing, but you probably don't know that they were following an earlier script. The abolition led by American writers and soldiers and British gunboats was the second round of major abolitionism and followed the first push by about eight hundred years.

St. Paul had endorsed both the rule of Rome, which was built on slavery, and the spiritual equality of all men. When he ran across an escaped slave, he all but promised the slave's Christian master that he would burn in hell if he didn't free him.[2] The medieval Catholic Church looked to his example and outlawed slavery in most of Europe. It was only the New World expansion of empires that brought slavery back.[3]

Critics could call Paul a hypocrite because he endorsed the *Pax Romana* but pursued a different and contradictory project within the early church, and worked to free at least one slave. And critics *have* called the American founders hypocrites for holding men in bondage even as they sought to throw off the shackles of British rule.

Historical context can be added to their actions, and we can pursue nuance into the wee hours. But for my dime, the only proper response is *so what?*

MANSON FAMILY FALLACIES

The point is that any judgment against hypocrisy should be a considered one. It should not be a default judgment. And we should think long and hard about whether we're willing to allow antihypocrites as reliable witnesses.

As I spoke to quite a lot of people during the writing of this book, one example kept cropping up, and I think the anti-hypocrites' knee jerk answer says, well, something.

The scenario was an example drawn from real life and a recent film: a pro-drug-war politician's daughter gets busted for possession of an illegal drug in a sufficient quantity to put her away for some time. Rather than denounce his own daughter, the politician hires a lawyer and twists a few arms. The girl is allowed by the prosecutor to plead to a charge of possession for a lesser amount of drugs than what was found on her, and the judge sentences her to six weeks of treatment in a detox facility.[4]

Cue the polemicists and political opponents, who cry hypocrisy. They ask why the politician wants people to be incarcerated for the same crime that almost sent his daughter into prison, and they try to use the issue to either undermine voter support for the pol or make a point about the war on drugs, or both.

The outcry seems unwise to me, and I said as much when I threw this story out there for other people to consider. Yes, it might have been hypocritical, but all the pol was doing was trying to protect his daughter. Who could object to that?

Plenty of people, it turned out. More than one questioned the family loyalty angle by likening the politician's clan to the Manson family. And what, they wanted to know, did I think of standing by a family of psycho killers?

A few more reasonable interlocutors argued that the politician should secure his daughter's release and then resign, as his actions had demonstrated his obvious hypocrisy and therefore his unfitness for public office. Unlike all those other people in public office.

I would continue to prod by saying that the outcry over hypocrisy here amounted to a procruelty position. If they wanted to turn this into a teachable moment, then critics should praise the politician for helping his kid out and then ask that he, and other pols, would extend that same understanding to other poor unfortunate souls who aren't as lucky as his daughter.

Further, I asked what would be accomplished by the man resigning. Ninety-nine point nine percent of American politicians want to "get tough on drugs" because voters want them to get tough on drugs. Take this pol out and he'll only be replaced by the next guy in the queue *who really means it* when he promises to break some heads.

But that's an argument for another day. Push the political issue to the side, if you can, and focus on the people. A father was trying to keep his own out of jail and get some help for her, and he was willing to put his credibility on the line to make this happen. The action was hypocritical, sure, but it was also normal and sane and even noble.

That's how it struck me anyway. The only question left is, how does it strike you?

THANKS

Thanks to Joel Miller for his encouragement and prodding. Without editors, I'm convinced most authors would starve. Thanks to Jim Antle for holding down the fort and to David Weigel for his research assistance. Thanks to the entire Lynden contingent, including the gorgeous gals at the Nuthouse. Thanks to the people who read all or part of the manuscript and gave feedback: Shawn Macomber, Wlady Pleszczynski, Thomas Pearson, Doug LeBlanc, Chuck Freund, Kristen Kestner, Greg Garner, Ryan Young, Jessie Creel, Patrick Basham, John Samples, Kevin Steel, KMG, Madison Kitchens, and David Boaz. The seed of chapter five first appeared in *Reason* magazine in the form of a book review, commissioned by Nick Gillespie and made readable by Jesse Walker. Thanks to Kelly Anne Creazzo for capturing me in that Mona Lisa-like pose on the book jacket. And thanks, finally, to Jamie Dettmer. He knows why.

NOTES

CHAPTER 1: Bill Bennett's Rap Sheet

1. Information in this section from both articles. Joshua Green, "The Bookie of Virtue," *Washington Monthly*, June 2003; Jonathan Alter and Joshua Green, "The Man of Virtues Has a Vice" *Newsweek*, May 12, 2003.

2. News Roundup, *Washington Times*, September 27, 1999.

3. Bennett's polemic *The Death of Outrage: Bill Clinton and the Assault on American Ideals* was written during this period, and published in September 1999.

4. Mark Whitaker, "The Editor's Desk," *Newsweek*, May 12, 2003.

5. Ian Mylchreest, "Casinos' conduct in question about Bennett disclosures," *Las Vegas Business Press*, May 9, 2003.

6. William J. Bennett interview on CNBC's *Tim Russert*, July 26, 2003.

7. Michael Kinsley, "Bill Bennett's Bad Bet," *Slate*, May 5, 2003, http://www. slate.com/id/2082526/.

8. From CNN's *Crossfire*, May 9, 2003. Said Begala, "Let's turn to the gospel, by the way, because there is a passage from the book of St. Matthews, particularly important for all of us to learn with Bill Bennett."

9. Katha Pollitt, "Bah, Humbug" (Subject to Debate column), *Nation*, June 2, 2003.

10. William F. Buckley, Jr., "Bennett and His Enemies," syndicated column, May 13, 2003.

11. *American Heritage Dictionary* (Houghton Mifflin, 2000).

12. Kinsley, "Bill Bennett's Bad Bet."

13. *Catechism of the Catholic Church* (Doubleday, 1995). Under Article 7: The Seventh Commandment, paragraph 2413 states, "Games of chance (card games, etc.) or wagers are not in themselves contrary to justice. They become morally unacceptable when they deprive someone of what is necessary to provide for his needs and those of others. The passion for gambling risks becoming an enslavement. Unfair wagers and cheating at games constitute grave matter, unless the damage inflicted is so slight that the one who suffers it cannot reasonably consider it significant."

14. Myriam Marquez, "If You're Peddling Virtue, You Can't Very Well Indulge in a Vice," *Orlando Sentinel,* May 11, 2003.

15. Ramesh Ponnuru, "In Defense of Hypocrisy," *Weekly Standard,* September 23, 1996.

16. Richard Gooding, "Top Clinton Aide and the Sexy Call Girl," *Star,* August 1996.

17. Ponnuru, "In Defense of Hypocrisy."

18. Ibid.

19. Author's transcription, *True Crime,* directed by Clint Eastwood, Warner Bros., 1999.

20. Peter Beinart, "Rules of the Game" (TRB from Washington column), *New Republic,* May 19, 2003.

CHAPTER 2: Conservatives and Cads

1. All quotes here are from Anton O. Kris, "The Lure of Hypocrisy," *Journal of American Psychoanalytic Association,* Issue 53/1, 2005, http://www.apsa. org/japa/531/Kris-pp.7-22.pdf.

2. Quotes in this section are from *Meet the Press,* NBC News

(transcript of interview with Howard Dean), May 22, 2005, http:// msnbc.msn.com/ id/7924139/.

3. Ron Chernow, *Alexander Hamilton* (Penguin 2004).

4. Justin Ewers, "The Real Lincoln," *U.S. News & World Report,* February 21, 2005.

5. Ronald D. Elving, "C-Span Gets Pushy," *CJR,* September/ October 1995.

6. Sandra Evans Teeley, "House Censures Crane and Studds," *Washington Post,* July 21, 1983.

7. *ABC's This Week,* October 20, 1990: "I will vote no on the conference package because it will be a recession increasing, job killing, tax increasing and deficit increasing package which I think is bad for America."

8. Tom Kentworthy, "Guess Who Bounced 8,331 Checks in 1 Year; Lawmakers Overdrew Accounts Without Penalty," *Washington Post,* September 20, 1992.

9. "House Bank Checks Out" (editorial), *Roll Call,* March 14, 2005.

10. "House Post Office Scandal," THOMAS information system, Library of Congress, July 21, 1993, http://icreport.loc.gov/cgi-bin/ query/z?r103: H21JY3-14.

11. "Republican Contract with America," United State House of Representatives Web site, http://www.house.gov/house/ Contract/CONTRACT.html.

12. Ibid.

13. David Pace, "Gingrich Promises to Lead Congress into New Era of Bipartisanship," Associated Press, November 9, 1994.

14. Benjamin Disraeli, speech on agricultural interests, March 17, 1845.

15. John E. Yang, "Gingrich to Pay Penalty with Dole Loan," *Washington Post,* April 18, 1997. "In December, Gingrich admitted he had brought discredit to the House and had broken its rules by

failing to ensure that financing for two projects, including a college course he once taught, would not violate federal tax law and by giving the ethics committee untrue information. In what amounted to a plea bargain, Gingrich agreed to a House reprimand and the financial penalty in exchange for reduced charges against him."

16. Peter Morgan and Glenn Reynolds, *The Appearance of Impropriety* (Free Press, 1997), 6.

17. Kris, "The Lure of Hypocrisy."

18. Susan Romero and Angela Scorza, "The Sunday Morning President vs. Saturday Night Bill," *Flux* (student paper of San Francisco State University), October 21, 1998. "I think that there are two Bill Clintons. There's a Sunday morning president and a Saturday night Bill. And the Sunday morning president doesn't recognize the existence of Saturday night Bill."

CHAPTER 3: Do as I Don't

1. This story drawn from both James Spiegel's book *How to Be Good in a World Gone Bad* (Kregel, 2005) and interview with the author, September 27, 2005.

2. Ruth W. Grant, *Hypocrisy and Integrity: Machiavelli, Rousseau, and the Ethics of Politics* (University of Chicago Press), 1997.

3. "I shall not today attempt further to define the kinds of material I understand to be embraced within that shorthand description; and perhaps I could never succeed in intelligibly doing so. But I know it when I see it, and the motion picture involved in this case is not that." Potter Stewart, from his concurring opinion in *Jacobellis v. Ohio* 378 U.S. 184 (1964).

4. "If I have on a short skirt, it doesn't mean that I have low morals. I have very high morals. I don't believe in sex before marriage. I don't believe in drugs or even smoking. I believe in God"; Britney Spears quote, "They Said What?" in *Observer* (UK), July 23, 2000.

5. David Nitkin, "First Lady's Comment Draws Criticism; She Joked about Shooting Britney Spears at Forum," *Baltimore Sun*, October 8, 2003.

6. Episode 102 (Season 6), "The Beard," *Seinfeld*, Sony Pictures Television.

7. François De La Rochefoucauld, *Maximes*, no. 218 (1678).

8. Niccolo Machiavelli, *The Prince*, (1513).

9. Henry Van Dyke, *The Story of the Other Wise Man* (Ballantine Books, 1996), xvi.

10. Exodus 1:15–16 (KJV): "And the king of Egypt spake to the Hebrew midwives, of which the name of one was Shiphrah, and the name of the other Puah: And he said, When ye do the office of a midwife to the Hebrew women, and see them upon the stools; if it be a son, then ye shall kill him: but if it be a daughter, then she shall live."

11. Adam Nicolson, *God's Secretaries: The Making of the King James Bible* (HarperCollins, 2003), 59.

12. Mason Locke Weems, *A History of the Life and Death, Virtues and Exploits of General George Washington*, 1918. From chapter 2: "'George,' said his father, 'do you know who killed that beautiful little cherry tree yonder in the garden?' This was a tough question; and George staggered under it for a moment; but quickly recovered himself: and looking at his father, with the sweet face of youth brightened with the inexpressible charm of all-conquering truth, he bravely cried out, 'I can't tell a lie, Pa; you know I can't tell a lie. I did cut it with my hatchet.' 'Run to my arms, you dearest boy,' cried his father in transports, 'run to my arms; glad am I, George, that you killed my tree; for you have paid me for it a thousand fold. Such an act of heroism in my son is more worth than a thousand trees, though blossomed with silver, and their fruits of purest gold.'"

13. Walker Percy, *Lancelot* (Picador, 1999), 92.

14. Strom Thurmond, inaugural address, January 21, 1947, in Columbia, South Carolina.

15. Jack Bass and Marilyn W. Thompson, *Ol' Strom: The Unauthorized Biography of Strom Thurmond* (University of South Carolina Press, 2003).

16. Ibid.

17. Harry G. Frankfurt, *On Bullshit* (Princeton University Press, 2005).

18. Béla Szabados and Eldon Soifer, *Hypocrisy: Ethical Investigations* (Broadview Press, 2004).

CHAPTER 4: Plank in Your Eye

1. Based on author's paraphrase of Matthew chapters 22 and 23.

2. William C. Symonds, "Earthy Empires," *Business Week*, May 23, 2005.

3. Rick Warren, *The Purpose-Driven Life* (Zondervan, 2002), 101.

4. Ibid., 162.

5. Jonathan McKee, "The Real Jaci Velasquez," The Source, http://www.thesource4ym.com/interviews/JaciVelasquez.asp.

6. Ibid., http://www.thesource4ym.com/archives/arc20030527.asp.

7. Matthew 7:2–5, author's paraphrase.

8. These stories can be found in Leviticus, chapter 10, and 1 Samuel, chapter 8.

9. John Jay College of Criminal Justice, "The Nature and Scope of the Problem of Sexual Abuse of Minors by Catholic Priests and Deacons in the United States" (a research study conducted March 2003–February 2004), posted on the Web site of the United States Conference of Catholic Bishops, http://www.usccb.org/nrb/john jaystudy/.

10. Matt Carroll, Sacha Pfeiffer, and Michael Rezendes, "Church Allowed Abuse by Priest for Years," *Boston Globe*, January 6, 2002.

11. "700 Priests Removed Since January 2002" (press release), United States Conference of Catholic Bishops, February 27, 2004, http://www.usccb.org/ comm/archives/2004/04-040.shtml.

12. Virginia de Leon, "Skylstad to Lead Bishops," *Spokesman-Review*, November 16, 2004.

13. John Wiley, "Spokane Diocese to File for Bankruptcy," Associated Press, November 10, 2004.

14. Ed Langlois, "Archdiocese of Portland Files Chapter 11 Bankruptcy," *Catholic Sentinel*, July 7, 2004.

15. Steve Woodward, "Archdiocese of Portland Parishes Will Join Dispute," *Oregonian*, July 1, 2005.

16. Jeff Wright, "Fight over Church's Assets Jabs Parishes," *Register-Guard*, September 29, 2005.

17. Ibid.

18. "$30 Million Award for Victims of Priest," Associated Press, July 17, 1998.

19. Brooks Egerton, "Judge in Kos Case Lets Emotions Out in Talk," *Dallas Morning News*, July 22, 1997.

20. Charol Shakeshaft, "Educator Sexual Misconduct: A Synthesis of Existing Literature," Department of Education, June 2004, http://www.ed.gov/rschstat/research/pubs/misconductreview/report.pdf.

21. From author's interview, February 17, 2006.

22. John Jay College, "The Nature and Scope of the Problem of Sexual Abuse."

23. "Grand Jury Flays Archdiocese for Hiding Priest Sex Abuse," *Morning Call* and wire reports, September 22, 2005.

24. Lynn Vincent, "Breaking Faith," *World*, March 30, 2002.

25. Kathy Shaidle, "OK, Just One . . ." Relapsed Catholic Web site, March 26, 2005, http://relapsedcatholic.blogspot.com/2005/03/ok-just-one.html.

CHAPTER 5: Walk the Talkies

1. "Edward Asner," Screen Actors Guild Presidents, SAG Web site, http://www.sag.org/history/presidents/asner.html.

2. "2004 Racism Watch Calls on Bush-Cheney Campaign to Change or Pull Offensive Ad—Spokesperson Ed Asner Asks if This Is the Beginning of a Disturbing Pattern" (press release), Common Dreams Newswire, March 31, 2004, http://www.common-dreams.org/news2004/0331-04.htm.

3. "Death Penalty," The Mobilization to Free Mumia Abu-Jamal, http:// www.freemumia.org/penalty.html.

4. David Tulanian, "Asner on Central America," *Los Angeles Times*, June 22, 1985.

5. "A Letter to the Peace and Justice Movement from Ed Asner," 9-11 Visibility Project, April 26, 2004, http://septembereleventh. org/alerts/ asner.php.

6. Jill Rosenfeld, "Giving Back," *Fast Company*, December 1999, http:// www.fastcompany.com/magazine/30/one.html.

7. Trey Parker, speaking at the U.S. Comedy Arts Festival, Aspen, CO, March 7, 1998.

8. Barbra Streisand, "The 'So-Called' Liberal Media," BarbraStreisand. com, December 10,2004,http://www.barbrastreisand.com/ statements.html.

9. Ibid.

10. Mitchell Fink and Lauren Rubin, "Apparently, Being John Cusack Means Being Really Mad at Bush," *New York Daily News*, June 7, 2001.

11. Ibid.

12. Rita Kempley, "Being John Cusack; The Young Actor Will Say Anything in an Interview. No Matter. His Work Speaks for Itself," *Washington Post*, July 15, 2001.

13. "John Stewart's Oscar Zingers," http://politicalhumor.about.com/.

14. Nick Gillespie and Steve Kurtz, "Stand-Up Guy" (interview), *Reason*, November 1997.

15. For voluminous evidence of this, see Aaron Tonken's *King of Cons: Exposing the Dirty Rotten Secrets of the Washington Elite and Hollywood Celebrities* (Nelson Current, 2004).

16. Peter Schweizer, *Do As I Say (Not As I Do): Profiles in Liberal Hypocrisy* (Doubleday, 2005).

17. Larissa MacFarquhar, "The Populist," *New Yorker*, February 16, 2004 and February 23, 2004.

18. Jesse Walker, "The War Between the Statists," Techcentralstation.com, November 8, 2004, http://www.tcsdaily.com/article.aspx?id=110804E.

19. Schweizer, *Do As I Say (Not As I Do)*.

20. The first, voluntary code of decency adopted by the Motion Picture Association of America, introduced in 1930 and named for former Postmaster General William Hays. It was strengthened in 1934, but abandoned in 1967.

21. Malcolm Gladwell, *Blink* (Little, Brown, 2005), 67-68.

22. "AFI's 100 Years . . .100 Lists," American Film Institute, AFI.com, http:// www.afi.com/tvevents/100years/100yearslist.aspx.

23. Author's transcription, *Casablanca*, directed by Michael Curtiz, Warner Bros., 1942.

24. Author's transcription, *Leap of Faith*, directed by Richard Pearce, Paramount Pictures, 1992.

CHAPTER 6: Hidden Hypocrisies

1. Elizabeth Mehran, "Nixon Aide Tells of Plan to Bomb Think Tank," *Los Angeles Times*, February 18, 2003.

2. From author's interview, November 1, 2005.

3. From author's interview, February 17, 2006.

4. Lynden Chamber of Commerce. See also http://www.lynden.org.

5. He was appointed to investigate the Whitewater scandal. See Michael Kranish, "Clinton Aides Lament New Special Counsel," *Boston Globe*, August 7, 1994.

6. John Aloysius Farrell, "White House Braces for Sex Suit Today," *Boston Globe*, May 5, 1994.

7. Richard Dooling, "Making Criminals of Us All," *New York Times*, December 30, 1998.

8. Mary Curtius, "Senators Want Outsiders for Ethics Overhaul," *Los Angeles Times*, January 26, 2006.

9. *Gonzales v. Oregon* (04-623) January 17, 2006.

CHAPTER 7: I, Hypocrite

1. Aldous Huxley, *Brave New World*, 1932.

2. See the book of Philemon.

3. For more on this, look to the work of sociologist Rodney Stark, particularly to *For the Glory of God: How Monotheism Led to Reformations, Science, Witch-Hunts, and the End of Slavery* (Princeton University Press, 2004).

4. *Traffic*, directed by Steven Soderburgh, Gramercy Pictures/USA Films, 2000.

INDEX